Gothic Style

Architecture and Interiors

from the

Eighteenth Century

to the

Present

KATHLEEN MAHONEY

PRINCIPAL PHOTOGRAPHY BY

MICHAEL DUNNE

ADDITIONAL PHOTOGRAPHS BY JOHN MAHONEY AND NIGEL HUDSON

HARRY N. ABRAMS, INC., PUBLISHERS

To the memory of our dear and treasured friend

Jack Macurdy

—K. M. and M. D.

Frontispiece: The round room at Strawberry Hill, with its stained-glass bay window and decorative dado, can be seen beyond the doorway at the far end of the long gallery. At each corner of the door frame are gilded quatrefoils with shields in their centers.

Endpapers: A 1763 engraving of King Alfred's Hall by Thomas Robins, believed to be the first Gothic sham ruin in England as well as one of the best. It was begun in 1721 on the estate of Lord Bathurst at Cirencester Park.

Editors: Beverly Fazio Herter and Elisa Urbanelli
Designers: Dirk Luykx and Amy Hill

Library of Congress Cataloging-in-Publication Data
Mahoney, Kathleen.
   Gothic style : architecture and interiors from the eighteenth century to the present
/ Kathleen Mahoney ; principal photography by Michael Dunne ; additional
photographs by John Mahoney and Nigel Hudson.
      p.   cm.
   Includes bibliographical references (p. 261–62).
   ISBN 0–8109–3381–0
   1. Gothic revival (Architecture)—England.   2. Decoration and ornament, Gothic
—England.   3. Interior decoration—England.   4. Gothic revival (Architecture)—
United States.   5. Decoration and ornament, Gothic—United States.   6. Interior
decoration—United States.   I. Title.
NA966.5.G66M326   1995
724'.3—dc20   94–32731

Published in 1995 by Harry N. Abrams, Incorporated, New York
A Times Mirror Company

Printed and bound in Japan

It is that strange disquietude of the Gothic spirit that is its greatness;

that restlessness of the dreaming mind, that wanders hither and thither

among the niches, and flickers feverishly around the pinnacles, and frets

and fades in labyrinthine knots and shadows along wall and roof,

and yet is not satisfied, nor shall be satisfied.

—JOHN RUSKIN, *THE STONES OF VENICE*

Contents

Introduction

RELEGATED TO THE DUSTY PAST, the Gothic style has languished for close to a hundred years, yet there are strong indications that a taste for Gothic, after a long hiatus, is resurfacing. Its return to favor promises an adventure into an imaginative world.

Two museum installations—a major exhibition sponsored by the Museum of Fine Arts, Houston, featuring decorative arts from the Gothic Revival period, plus the addition of a Gothic Revival room at New York City's Metropolitan Museum of Art—undoubtedly provided added impetus. These days, as prices for antique Gothic treasures climb, sending collectors scrambling, designers and architects are increasingly turning to Gothic's rich design heritage for inspiration. Gothic designs are turning up in a wide assortment of home furnishings, from furniture, fabric, and wall coverings to decorative objects and architectural applications in houses, conservatories, and even skyscrapers.

Yet for many today, the Gothic Revival is little understood, calling to mind dark, slightly sinister Victorian interiors or novels recounting tales of horror. In truth, these manifestations played but a small role in a major, emotionally charged movement that persisted for more than a century, stretching across national boundaries from England and its colonies into Europe, Russia, Scandinavia, and America. Gothic ultimately was to influence virtually all creative endeavors, none more so than the decorative arts and architecture.

Elements of Gothic style, the roots of which reach back to medieval times, never really stopped being used for simple English dwellings. In addition, the need for constant repair to early churches required a working knowledge of Gothic on the part of stone masons, whose skills had been handed down from one generation to the next. Universities, such as Oxford and Cambridge, and churches continued to be constructed and expanded upon in the original Gothic style, frequently for the sake of continuity of tradition. These buildings, the product of surviving Gothic influences, bore a great similarity to those erected several hundred years earlier.

However, the introduction and development of Gothic as an expression of the Romantic Movement was quite another story. Its early-eighteenth-century revival was marked by a decidedly new form, which emerged as a release from classical restraints. It was exuberant, borrowing Gothic elements in a whimsical, lighthearted manner. From mock ruins and other fanciful garden follies to flamboyant manor-house interiors, its inventive and decidedly playful approach was purely decorative and evocative. Enthusiasts found joy simply in what pleased the eye, as they incorporated motifs from original Gothic structures, imaginatively adapting whatever suited their fancy. Freed from the classical formality in vogue at the time, Gothic motifs offered endless variety.

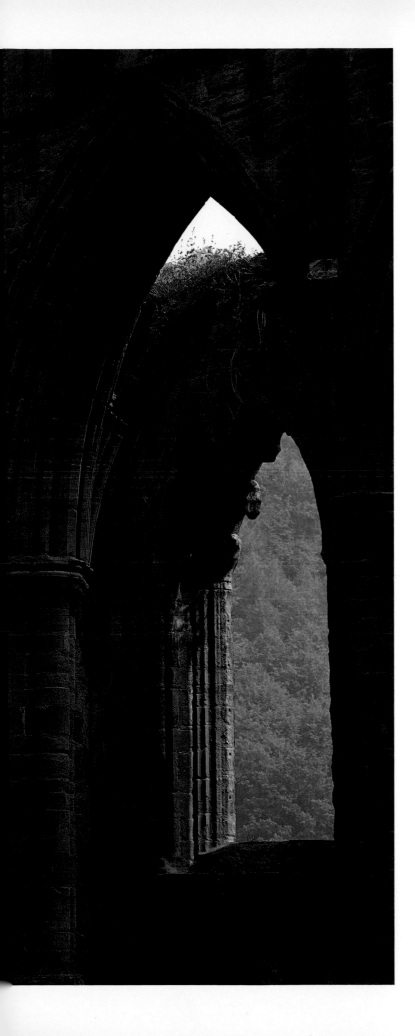

The reappearance of Gothic in the eighteenth century was brought about in part by a fascination with the legends and lore of medieval times. Ballads written during the Middle Ages became extremely popular and were a source of inspiration for creative spirits of the day, who were captivated by notions of knighthood and chivalry. The dark side of the Middle Ages was particularly exciting to poets and writers, who delved into the mysterious and the supernatural with great abandon. This fascination was largely responsible for the building of castles during the last quarter of the eighteenth and into the nineteenth century.

In the third decade of the nineteenth century the character of Gothic changed profoundly, shifting to a more serious approach guided by the Ecclesiologists, a powerful group whose aim was the reform of church architecture, and by the religious dogmatism of architect A. W. N. Pugin. Gothic style became imbued with moral and religious meaning, with devotees emphasizing structural honesty and archaeological accuracy. By the beginning of Queen Victoria's reign in 1837, Gothic was entrenched in England, moving toward a heavy, more ornate expression typical of the period.

Across the Atlantic, a new nation devoid of its own historical references turned to England for guidance in style trends. America was prospering as the nineteenth century evolved, shedding its Colonial garb and venturing to explore a variety of architectural styles. Under the guidance of architect A. J. Davis and landscape gardener and writer A. J. Downing, Gothic forms bloomed across the American landscape. Exuberant manifestations appeared in the guise of cottages and villas enlivened by the

Just across the Welsh border, on the right bank of the River Wye, sits the still remains of Tintern Abbey, confiscated by King Henry VIII in 1536. The picturesque site became a popular tourist attraction in the eighteenth century.

liberal use of the jigsaw. Steeply pitched gables gaily trimmed with lacy vergeboards and decorative bay and oriel windows extending from façades gave a storybook look to houses. Castle-like residences, while less popular in the States than in England, nevertheless made an appearance, especially along the picturesque banks of the Hudson River.

The term Gothic Revival was first used around 1850 and became accepted with the 1872 publication of Charles Eastlake's *A History of the Gothic Revival*. In America it is generally applied to the entire period from the eighteenth century through its late-nineteenth-century decline. The English, however, distinguish between stylistic periods, adopting the spelling Gothick when referring to the exuberant eighteenth-century influences, as writers at the time commonly did, and Gothic Revival to denote only the later, more serious nineteenth-century forms. I have chosen to use Gothick as the English do in order to clearly distinguish between the two very different stylistic trends.

For citizens of the eighteenth century, putting a name to this eccentric, budding style was something of a problem. The word Gothic conjured up visions of the Visigoths, who overran Europe from the third to the fifth centuries, bringing about an end to the Roman Empire. Controversy about the nomenclature raged throughout the eighteenth century, as alternate names such as Pointed, Christian, and English were suggested. The term Gothic seems to have actually originated in sixteenth-century Italy, where design influences based on the precepts of classical Roman architecture were faithfully adhered to. Italians looked disdainfully upon anything not classical, thinking of it as barbaric. A seventeenth-century dictionary defined Gothic as anything crude or rough.

With the study of history still in a primitive state in the eighteenth century, Gothic's twelfth-century origins were vague to most. Some, like writers

Goethe, Hegel, and Coleridge, believed the Gothic cathedral to be inspired by the crossing of branches in a forest, while others were convinced it was a style brought back from the Crusades of the twelfth century.

The original Gothic style actually evolved from the Romanesque and had its beginnings in France at the church of St. Denis just outside Paris, the construction of which was begun in 1140. It was the parts of the church to be completed last—the choir, aisles, and chapels, distinguished by their pointed arches and ribbed vaults—that were distinctly Gothic. Less than one hundred years later, with the building of Chartres in 1220, the Gothic style was to reach its zenith.

What made this style unique was the way it handled architectural stress. With arches designed to push against each other, stone walls, stabilized by reinforcements in the form of exposed flying buttresses, climbed to heights never before reached. Another outstanding quality of Gothic was its extraordinary use of light. As the style developed, walls became mere shells to house vast expanses of luminescent stained-glass windows, which flooded church interiors with multifaceted rays of light. These masterpieces of architecture also employed vaulted ceilings, pinnacles, tracery, and decorative details such as crockets and gargoyles related to nature or to the grotesque; all were united into a

Romsey Abbey, c. 1220.

Meopham, Kent, c. 1280.

Rushden, Northamptonshire, c. 1500.

symbiotic union of design and structure.

While Roche Abbey (c. 1160) is credited as the first Gothic building in England, a more fully developed Gothic style appeared just fifteen years later, with the replacement of the choir destroyed by fire at the legendary Norman Canterbury Cathedral. French influences continued in England, especially at Canterbury and Westminster Abbey, but before long the English developed a style entirely their own. Rejecting the soaring heights of the French cathedrals and their lavish use of carved ornamentation, the English elected instead to elongate, replacing a grouping of chapels with a square east end and adding a transept positioned almost in the center, with an occasional smaller second transept. Interiors were frequently divided into compartments.

Gothic architecture eventually made its way from ecclesiastical buildings to residences, civil buildings, and colleges, such as Oxford and Cambridge, established in the twelfth century, and the public schools Winchester and Eton, founded in 1387 and 1440, respectively. This design tradition stretches into the twentieth century, as many col-

leges and universities still look to those early halls of learning for architectural inspiration.

Gothic reigned supreme throughout the Middle Ages. Like all design movements that endure over a broad period of time, as it evolved it manifested elements that were generally characteristic of a particular stage. Historian Thomas Rickman, in his 1819 handbook, *An Attempt to Discriminate the Styles of Architecture in England from the Conquest to the Reformation,* divided medieval architecture into four periods, establishing names for each still in use today. It was to bring Gothic a step closer to gaining academic respectability at the time.

The first, which started with the reign of William I and the Norman Conquest in 1066, was appropriately called Norman. It was the second period, referred to by Rickman as Early English, that marked the beginnings of Gothic. Characterized by the use of narrow lancet windows and clustered columns, Early English began around 1189, as Richard I assumed the throne, extending until 1280.

The transition from one phase to another was a

gradual one. The use of bar tracery, consisting of branching ribs or mullions in windows, allowing them to be made considerably larger, was first introduced in France at Reims Cathedral in 1211 and was quickly adopted by the English during what Rickman termed the Decorated period, which followed roughly one hundred years after the start of Early English. An important step in the evolution of Gothic, the subdivision of windows, now an essential part of the structure, ultimately progressed to the point where walls diminished to mere skeletal forms. It was during this period that ornament became more naturalistic and less restricted to structural use.

By the fourteenth century, the Continent was moving toward the Renaissance. The Hundred Years' War between England and France raged from 1337 to 1453 and resulted in England's loss of all its French possessions save for Calais. Coupled with Henry VIII's battles with the papacy sometime later, England was cut off from much of Catholic Europe, prolonging the use of Gothic. The Perpendicular Style, which evolved during this time, was uniquely English. Its emphasis was on verticality and the use of light. Window tracery became rectangular, ornamented with simple cusping. The decorative fan vault and elaborate paneled walls, which we will see adapted in a number of beautiful manor houses of the eighteenth century, were introduced. Many older cathedrals were the recipients of graceful new towers.

The Tudor style, characterized by flat centered arches used over doors and windows and elaborate vaulting, was considered the last phase of the Perpendicular period, running from about 1485 to 1555. It, too, was restricted to England. While not a period of great church building, a number of beautiful chapels, such as the one at King's College, Cambridge, were built during this time.

In 1534 King Henry VIII retaliated against the pope for refusing to declare his marriage to his first wife invalid. The King was appointed head of the Church of England by Parliament, establishing an independent national Anglican Church and the start of the English Reformation. Two years later, land owned by the Catholic church was confiscated by the Crown. While some of England's great country houses were subsequently built on the foundations of dispossessed old Catholic abbeys, a number of Gothic churches were left to ruin, and by the eighteenth century all that remained of the once vastly powerful structures were skeletal forms made up of crumbling arches and walls.

To the romantic-minded eighteenth-century English tourists, these Gothic ruins were looked upon as wonderfully picturesque and melancholic. One of the most popular of the solitary sites to visit was the Cistercian Tintern Abbey in Wales, which proved to be a source of inspiration for eighteenth-century artists and writers such as J. M. W. Turner, one of the most important painters of his time, and the then-popular travel writer the Reverend William Gilpin, who wrote of Tintern, "Mosses of various hues, with lychens, maiden hair, penny-leaf, and other humble plants, overspread the surface . . . all together they give these full-blown tints which add the richest finishing to a ruin." Semblances of ruins recalling the melancholy remains of these early feats of architecture were soon to grace lush English gardens. Decidedly whimsical, they were to become the first step in the revival of Gothic.

By the sixteenth century the Renaissance had brought neoclassicism into the mainstream of design throughout much of Europe, but it was not until the first quarter of the seventeenth century that the Renaissance came to England, spearheaded by leading English architect Inigo Jones. It was the rebellion against these forms a century later that ultimately motivated the return of Gothic. Once

This overall view of Tintern Abbey, a medieval monastery settled by monks of the Cistercian order, faces toward the Presbytery, which housed the church's high altar. The east end of the 236-foot-long church is on the far right.

ensconced, Gothic went on to dominate design throughout much of the nineteenth century.

Because of the vast scope of the movement, I have elected to concentrate on Gothic's more light-hearted aspects, found in the early days of its reappearance in the British Isles and its subsequent entry into America, with a brief look at mid-nineteenth-century English adaptations for comparison, and, finally, to trace its intriguing journey into the twentieth century with a closing glance at recent interpretations.

For those of you who are unfamiliar with the Gothic Revival, it is my hope that you will find as much pleasure in the discovery of Gothic as I did

when I first came across pictures of Horace Walpole's Strawberry Hill. I was drawn to its fantasy and its delight in the unexpected and in short order found myself delving into books on the subject to learn more about this remarkable period, which was sadly neglected in my art history classes. For those of you who have already been initiated into this energetic, eccentric style, it is my wish that my book will afford some undiscovered insights and a greater appreciation of Gothic.

I have provided a glossary at the back of the book for clarification of architectural terms and a bibliography that lists recent relevant books and early manuscripts for those who have an interest in pursuing the subject further.

Part I

The English Landscape Garden

Green House.

HROUGHOUT the seventeenth century and well into the eighteenth, grandly formal English houses were looked upon as the height of fashion. Situated in parks whose design dictates were governed by the same precepts, their vast gardens stretched out in symmetrical precision, with arbors, parterres, and plantings clipped to within an inch of their lives. As the eighteenth century progressed, however, a totally new spirit swept the country, first surfacing in the verdant gardens of English estates. The mood shifted away from the reserved formality brought about by classical restraints toward a decidedly exuberant romanticism.

Irregular plantings simulating unspoiled nature began replacing formal gardens, as master gardeners worked with nature in the same manner an artist would a canvas. In their attempt to create an earthly paradise, garden designers scattered trees and shrubbery throughout rolling hillsides that were dotted by man-made lakes, meandering streams, and waterfalls. These picturesque inventions virtually redefined the garden. Since it was no longer sufficient to simply be pleasing to the eye, gardens were now laid out in an effort to evoke a multitude of sensations, especially one of agreeable melancholy. To a country bound by the limitations of earlier formality, the illusion of unrestrained nature was deliciously seductive.

Fueled by the works of literary and artistic talents of the day, the voice of reason was replaced by a force that delighted in the senses and the emotions. These new attitudes proved to be fertile soil for a style as eccentric as Gothick. With its link to nature, its boldness, and its brooding melancholy, Gothick was a natural expression of the country's budding romantic mood. Encouraging inventiveness, its exuberant form provided an escape from classical tradition. The early high-spirited, decorative eighteenth-century interpretations, referred to as Georgian Gothick, rococo, and Strawberry Hill Gothic, were less concerned with historical accuracy than they were with evoking a mood.

Many credit the multitalented William Kent with formulating the concept of the landscape garden. Gothick luminary Horace Walpole described Kent as "painter enough to taste the charms of landscape, bold and opinionative enough to dare and to dictate, and born with a genius to strike out a great system from the twilight of imperfect essays."[1] A major influence on Kent and other designers came from landscape paintings of seventeenth-century French artists Claude Lorrain and Nicolas Poussin, and the

Italian Salvator Rosa, which were brought back as souvenirs by well-bred young gentlemen who undertook the Grand Tour throughout Europe as an essential part of their education.

Contemporary writer Kelli Pryor aptly describes the works of artists Poussin and Lorrain. "Nicolas Poussin created memorials to human virtue in which the land was every bit as heroic as the mythological figures that inhabited it. At the same time, his fellow countryman Claude Lorrain explored the countryside around Rome, painting expansive pastoral idylls caught in the honeyed light of early morning or late afternoon. His gentle nostalgia for a golden age, one in which human and natural forms coexisted harmoniously, holds a special appeal. . . ."[2]

Kent's image of a garden was one unencumbered by boundaries; it was made possible with the introduction of ha-ha's, ditches surrounding country houses, reinforced by stones and bricks that were constructed to confine animals to the adjoining fields, thus allowing fences, walls, and other visible

The Section of MERLIN's CAVE in the Royal Gardens at Richmond.
as Design'd by Mr. Kent. I. Vardy delin. et sculp.

This engraving shows a section of Merlin's cave at Richmond, designed by William Kent for Queen Caroline in 1733 and published in 1744 in J. Vardy, Some Designs of Mr. Inigo Jones and Mr. William Kent.

means of enclosure to be eliminated. Walpole believed that ha-ha's were a decisive element in the evolution of the informal garden and related in his essay, *On Modern Gardening*, that they were "an attempt then deemed so astonishing that the common people called them Ha-Ha's! to express their surprize at finding a sudden and unperceived check to their walk."[3] Once ha-ha's were in place, the distant hills and valleys of the surrounding countryside became visual extensions of picturesque landscape gardens.

Kent, who had little experience in garden planning, operated purely on intuition. His informal garden designs may have been influenced by travelers' engravings of Chinese gardens, featuring serpentine paths and grottoes interspersed with patches of wilderness. The beautiful garden of Rousham in Oxfordshire, laid out around 1740 to incorporate a series of picturesque vistas, is the only garden design of Kent's that has survived unaltered. Kent's first garden commission was at Chiswick, a family estate of his mentor, Lord Burlington, where the two collaborated in the 1729 design of an immense and irregular garden. Kensington, one of many garden commissions that followed for Kent, "even had dead trees planted in it to heighten the similarity to Salvator's landscapes," as writer Christopher Hussey noted in his book *The Picturesque*.[4]

The versatile Kent also occasionally employed Gothic motifs for garden structures, such as in his 1733 design of Merlin's cave, a thatched Gothick folly built in Richmond Park, now known as Kew Gardens. It was demolished in 1764, when landscape gardener Capability Brown replaced the formal gardens.

The paintings of the seventeenth-century artists frequently included a distant classical ruin to catch the eye, and before long similar structures punctuated English estates. These seemingly decaying castles, referred to as sham ruins, lent an air of mystery and melancholy to newly developed land-

Sanderson Miller's sham ruin castle was inspired by the battle of Edge Hill fought on the site. Constructed in 1745 on a ridge, it provided wonderful views of the countryside and functioned as an eye-catcher for Radway Grange. (1862 engraving by G. Walford)

scape gardens. The deceptive buildings were not only designed to look like remnants from an earlier civilization, they were also built to give the appearance of being constructed of stone when in fact they were frequently made of wood and covered with plaster or canvas.

It was only natural for English gardeners to include Gothic as well as classical ruins as eye-catchers in their romantic picturesque gardens. With the dissolution of the Catholic Church by Henry VIII in the early sixteenth century, many Gothic abbeys and priories were left to ruin. Coupled a century later with Cromwell's plundering of Tudor country houses during England's civil war, authentic Gothic ruins abounded throughout the countryside. When proximity permitted, real monastic ruins such as those at Rievaulx, Fountains, and Roche were actually incorporated into adjoining gardens, capitalizing on their evocative and decorative qualities. Lord Kames was among those who preferred the Gothick style for sham ruins. In his 1762 *Elements of Criticism*, he commented, "Gothic

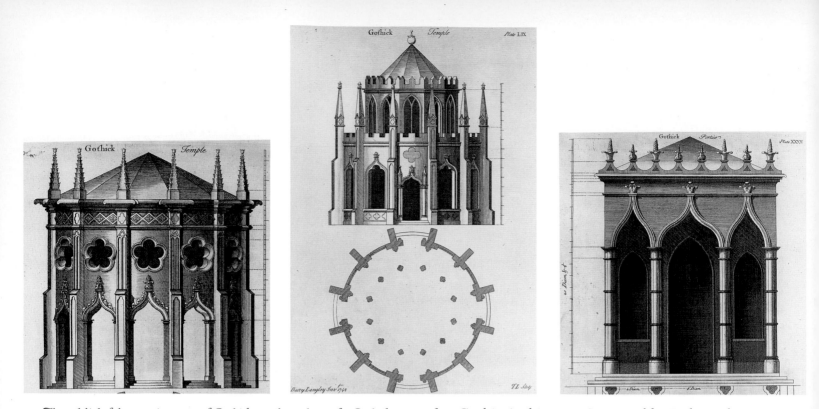

Three delightful engravings, two of Gothick temples and one of a Gothick portico, from Gothic Architecture Improved by Rules and Proportions, *the 1742 pattern book by Batty and Thomas Langley, which was instrumental in encouraging the use of Gothick for garden buildings.*

exhibits the triumph of time over strength; a melancholy, but not unpleasant thought; a Grecian ruin suggests rather the triumph of barbarity over taste; a gloomy discouraging thought."[5]

One of the first of these intriguing ruined castles was Alfred's Hall, first built in 1721 and enlarged in 1732 on the magnificent grounds of Cirencester Park by the first Earl of Bathurst. Bathurst was a close friend of poet Alexander Pope, an early crusader for liberating orderly gardens, who, in a 1713 essay in *The Guardian*, wrote, "There is certainly something in the amiable Simplicity of unadorned Nature, that spreads over the Mind a more noble sort of Tranquility, and a loftier Sensation of Pleasure, than can be raised from the nicer Scenes of Art."[6] In his own three-and-a-half-acre garden in Twickenham, Pope abandoned parterres and avenues, replacing them with a broad vista enclosed by woodland that was interrupted by serpentine walks and a hidden grotto.

Another early Gothick luminary was Sanderson Miller, a wealthy gentleman architect whose talents were frequently called upon in the adaptation of Gothick. In 1745 he designed a sham ruin for himself in the form of a Gothick tower, with heraldic shields, stained glass, and even a nonfunctioning drawbridge. Its hilltop spot near a picturesque thatched cottage he had built the previous year in the village of Edge Hill afforded a pleasant view of the surrounding countryside and functioned as a distant eye-catcher from his Radway Grange estate below. In short order it became a tourist attraction, establishing Miller's reputation for the design of ruins. Not long after its completion Miller was commissioned by Sir George Lyttelton to build a ruined castle in his expansive Hagley Park near Stourbridge (see page 25).

Miller's more important Gothick contributions included the 1755 addition of a splendid Gothick entrance hall at Lacock Abbey and early restoration efforts at his friend Roger Newdigate's fantastic Arbury Hall, where he is believed to have executed several two-story bay windows with cusped paneling, an architectural embellishment for which Miller became known (see page 111).

As the century progressed, garden buildings of great variety, referred to collectively as follies, became increasingly popular as whimsical adornments scattered about the landscape. Some were positioned on hilltops with sweeping vistas of picturesque gardens below or at the edge of man-made lakes, their decorative façades charmingly reflected in the tranquil water; many were placed at the end of garden paths, while others were tucked away in a secret grove waiting to delight the discoverer. It was in the design of these fanciful garden structures that the Gothic Revival had its beginnings.

Designs for these decorative garden structures were frequently copied from pattern books, which were influential in encouraging trends. Inexpensive and readily available, pattern books proliferated throughout the eighteenth and nineteenth centuries, specializing in such subjects as architecture, furniture design, and garden planning.

The first to suggest and illustrate Gothick buildings for gardens in a pattern book was a sometime architect and gardener by the unlikely name of Batty Langley, who, in response to growing interest in Gothick, published *Gothic Architecture Improved by Rules and Proportions. In Many Grand Designs* in 1742 with his brother Thomas. It contained a total of sixty-four delightful engravings of temples, "umbrellos," fireplaces, windows, doorways, and pavilions, confections dreamed up by Langley that only vaguely resembled their medieval ancestry. It also included five "Gothick Orders" that Langley invented, based on those found in classical design, in his attempt to make Gothic conform to prevailing classical standards.

Langley's unique designs were decorative as well as innovative and were responsible to a large extent for the development of a style that in its early stages

became known as the Batty Langley Manner. The double-curved ogee arch prominently featured in his pattern book was one of its major characteristics. A prolific writer with more than twenty publications to his name, Langley had been one of the first to advocate the use of ruins to end garden walks, in a 1728 publication, *Principles of Gardening.*

His many design books were extremely popular, and, like a number of design books of the day, *Gothic Architecture Improved* carried a list of supporters; the illustrious group included bishops, judges, and members of the nobility. Among them was Horace Walpole. Walpole, however, engrossed in the world of antiquity, considered his vision of Gothick far superior to Langley's free interpretation. He disdained Langley's original approach because Langley presumed to improve upon authentic forms in an attempt to update the style for eighteenth-century tastes. Walpole's villa, Strawberry Hill, brought his own personal interpretation of Gothick to reality a decade later (see page 101). Interestingly, some of its early exterior renovations bear a great similarity to designs featured in Langley's book.

By mid-century, garden follies had become an essential element in English garden design, frequently providing a visual connection to the main house as well as a melancholic reference. The lively forms of Gothick, adapted for a significant number of garden structures, sparked the imagination of architects and landowners, leading to further experimentation.

By the end of the eighteenth century, with the growth of the Picturesque Movement, which espoused the adoption of a painterly approach to gardens, garden buildings as well as manor houses were looked upon primarily as elements within a composition. Their placement was established based on their pictorial effect upon a scene.

Hagley Park

SHAM RUIN

HAGLEY HALL IS SURROUNDED by one of the great Worcestershire gardens; its immense private park, consisting of several small woods and pools scattered across rolling hillsides, is an early example of a picturesque landscape garden.

The first Lord Lyttelton, who was responsible for Hagley Hall's eighteenth-century restoration, was a man of diverse interests; involved in politics, he served for a year as the prestigious Chancellor of the Exchequer. He was also a poet and historian with a large number of literary friends, including Henry Fielding, whose novel *Tom Jones* was dedicated to him. Horace Walpole was a friend as well.

Lyttelton had originally wanted Sanderson Miller to redesign his 1564

Opposite: This intriguing eye-catcher embellishing the extensive grounds of Hagley Park, designed by "gentleman" architect Sanderson Miller in 1747, is a prime example of a sham ruin, one of the first structures to punctuate eighteenth-century landscape gardens.

Above: A detail of the sham ruin wall.

Below: Designed to be viewed from a distance and to suggest medieval origins, the seemingly decaying castle, sheltered by a large sycamore, was partly constructed of stones and architectural elements taken from an authentic thirteenth-century abbey that lay in ruin nearby.

family house in the Gothick style, but with considerable persuasion from his wife, he finally elected to build a Palladian mansion executed by Miller. Completed in 1760, Hagley Hall was the last of the great Palladian houses in England.

In keeping with the fashion of the day, Lyttelton built a collection of follies throughout his grounds. Dispersed about were a Doric temple, an Ionic rotunda, an obelisk, and a ruined castle situated on what Walpole described as "a hill of three miles, but broke into all manner of beauty."[7] When Lyttelton saw the sham ruin Sanderson Miller had designed for himself at Radway Grange, he wanted one as well.

Miller's ruin in Hagley Park was constructed in 1747 and placed at Lyttelton's request on a "prominent hill to be seen from the house and to appear as though it has survived from medieval times." From its hilltop, the Black Mountains of Wales, about forty miles away, can be seen on a clear day. Rose Macaulay, in her informative book *Pleasure of Ruins,* notes that a visitor to it recalled how when climbing the hill "your eye will, delighted, repose . . . on the remains of an old dusty building, solemn and venerable, rearing its gothic turret among the bushy trees."[8] Walpole had commented that the make-believe fortress, whose crumbling walls were covered with ivy and lichen, had "the true rust of the Barons' Wars."[9]

Partially built of sandstone and inset with pointed window frames from the ruined thirteenth-century Halesowen Abbey nearby, the whimsical structure is more than seventy feet long, with one whole tower and three partial ones. It is believed that Lyttelton had originally planned to use the sham ruin for entertaining because Miller had been requested to design chairs for it. The delicate Gothick plasterwork in the top room of the completed tower confirms this.

Recently the sham ruin has undergone extensive restoration undertaken by a tenant who was seduced by its fanciful charm. The beautiful Palladian Hagley Hall is now the home of Viscount Cobham and, along with its surrounding park, is open to the public in January, February, and August.

Above: The main tower of Hagley Park's sham ruin, four stories high and thirteen feet in diameter, was originally used as a gamekeeper's lodge. Now leased to a lawyer, the diminutive castle serves as his country house.

Below: Three shorter towers, one shown here, were used for a larder, bakehouse, and stables.

Enville

SUMMER HOUSE

Above: The flamboyant curves topping the front façade of the recently restored summer house are repeated over the doorway and its flanking windows. This delightful folly, about twenty-four feet deep, has been referred to throughout the years as a billiard room and a museum.

Opposite: The decorative Gothick windows of the summer house at Enville are positioned between clustered columns that visually divide the façade into thirds. Subtle blocks of pointed arches run across at midpoint.

ONE OF THE MOST ENCHANTING of eighteenth-century garden structures is a Gothick summer house at Enville, a large estate in Staffordshire adjacent to Hagley Park. Enville's eighteenth-century owner, Lord Stamford, filled its spacious grounds with a dazzling array of delightful follies.

A number of Enville's follies, such as a boathouse, farmhouse, and arch, were Gothic in design. A nineteenth-century addition included a spectacular Gothic glass conservatory 160 feet long. One of few that has survived the passage of time is the recently restored summer house, believed to have originally been used as a billiard room and later as a small museum. An eighteenth-century letter mentions "an exceedingly, well designed

Right and below: One of the few remaining follies on the Enville estate, this summer house was once one of many on the grounds built during the eighteenth century as adornments to the landscape. Ogee arches, edged with small crockets, frame the top of the center door and a pair of side windows ornamented with large quatrefoils.

Gothick Billiard Room" at Enville that included a billiard table, an organ, and busts of Homer and Cicero. Mr. R. Fish, gardener at Putteridge Bury, in an article featured in the 1864 edition of *The Journal of Horticulture and Cottage Gardener*, refers to the summer house as a museum. "Of the museum itself, though we took a few notes, we must say nothing of its birds, and fishes, and animals, and shells, and fossils, and ores, and minerals, and kinds of rocks, but from its pinnacled turrets, and pretty oriel windows, and its position on a knoll, and its background of trees and evergreens, it forms a fine feature to the grounds from many distinct points of view."[10]

Sanderson Miller designed several follies here for the Earl of Stamford and might possibly have been responsible for the summer house. Some, however, believe it is the work of Henry Keene. Its charm-

ing ogee arches and rose windows are similar to Keene's lovely Hartwell church in Buckinghamshire, one of the few rococo Gothick churches designed during this time.

Situated in a clump of trees not far from the main house, the Batty Langley–style summer house can be seen across the manicured lawn from the dining room and the master bedroom windows. Its outstanding architectural feature is its triple ogee-shaped arches, trimmed with finials and crockets, that form the top of its front façade. This lyrical ogee shape is repeated atop the central door, which most probably had a finial at its apex, and on the two small windows flanking it.

Decorative clustered columns run up the façade and join the inner ends of the top ogee arches, dividing the building visually into thirds. In the central section a large, round, flower-like painted-glass window is joined by two smaller ones on either side.

About twenty-four feet deep, the summer house's interior, once elaborately decked out in fanciful plasterwork, is still in need of restoring. A decorative fireplace flanked by windows is centered on the back wall; side walls are ornamented with three delicate plaster ogee-shaped arches, the central ones carved out to form niches. A suggestion of a plaster molding just under the ceiling remains.

Sold about fifteen years ago, Enville is now managed by the Trustees of Enville Estate. Recently a grant from English Heritage, coupled with a generous contribution from Enville's present owner, has enabled repair to be undertaken by William Hawkes, an authority on Sanderson Miller.

Painshill Park

GOTHICK TEMPLE

AND

SHAM RUIN

Opposite: Painshill Park's recently rebuilt sham ruin is in need of weathering and vegetation climbing its pristine walls to give it the desired appearance of an authentic ruin.

LANDSCAPE GARDENS became extremely popular by the mid-eighteenth century. While many of the most outstanding ones, such as Stowe and Stourhead, were the creations of professional gardeners, the beautiful Painshill Park in Cobham, Surrey, was designed by its owner, the Honorable Charles Hamilton, an inspired horticulturist. Hamilton possessed the imagination of an artist and incorporated this with a love of the unexpected in the design of his park. One of the most splendid of eighteenth-century gardens, Painshill combined carefully contrived landscaping, designed for optimum visual effect, with winding circuit walks typical of the picturesque gardens inspired by the growing Romantic Movement.

Hamilton purchased a lease in 1738 for 250 acres that were formerly part of a deer park owned by Henry VII. During the following thirty-five years he transformed the barren heath into one of the finest and best-known gardens in England. Painshill was one of the first gardens to include an assemblage of plants from the American colonies.

Many traveled to Painshill to enjoy Hamilton's creation. At each turn along the serpentine three-mile walk, visitors were treated to a variety of pleasant discoveries. Areas were divided up into scenes, some featuring nature at its wildest and others the serenity of open parkland surrounded by clusters of trees. Throughout the journey, an eclectic collection of fanciful structures unexpectedly presented themselves and then, a bit farther along, disappeared from view. Plantings visible from each vista were selected for color, texture, and shape and were carefully positioned as on elaborate stage sets. A Gothick temple, a Turkish tent, a temple of Bacchus, a Chinese bridge, and, at the edge of a pond, a sham ruin in the form of a Gothic abbey all played a part in Hamilton's elaborate scheme. Each appeared and then was gone until the finale, when visitors could catch sight of many of the follies at the same time.

Lack of funds forced Hamilton to sell his beloved park in 1773. Miraculously, it survived the following 150 years intact, until it was purchased in 1948 by a land speculator who started to subdivide it and sell off plots. Fortunately, the Eldridge town council, urged by a group of concerned locals, came to its rescue, recovering 158 of Painshill Park's original 250 acres. Subsequently, a number of other support groups have lent their assistance, including the English Heritage and the Prince of Wales, who has become its Royal Patron. Major restoration efforts started in 1981 with the founding of an independent trust, which embarked on extensive research to determine Hamilton's original plan; descriptions from early visitors were especially helpful. The Gothick temple and the sham ruin shown here were the first to be restored. Painshill Park has recently reopened to the public.

At the end of a heavily wooded path not far from the entrance to Painshill Park, this Gothick temple appears like a crown upon the landscape.

Painswick

ROCOCO GARDEN

Right: Painswick's gardens are approached by descending a winding path down to a broad lawn. Shortly before rounding the first bend, a tiny hexagonal Gothick temple appears at the edge of the path. Upon the next turn, one discovers that it alights atop the Eagle House, one of a number of fanciful follies scattered around the grounds.

Opposite: The tiny Red House to the far right of a broad expanse of lawn is unusual in its asymmetrical shape. Designed to be viewed from the front, its architectural interest is concentrated on its garden façade. The interior bears the Hyett family coat of arms and the motto "A steadfast heart."

IN THE SCENIC VILLAGE of Painswick on the edge of the Cotswolds in Gloucestershire is a lovely six-acre estate. Built on a hillside, Painswick's hidden garden, a mix of both formal and informal elements, is tucked away behind the main Georgian house. Its broad central lawn, interrupted by two small ponds, a bowling green, and a kitchen garden, is bordered by serpentine paths and woodland walks, with a number of decorative garden structures, mostly Gothick in design, scattered throughout.

Some of its delightful follies, like the tiny asymmetrical Gothick Red House on the edge of the grounds and a Gothick pavilion, named, for some unknown reason, the Eagle House, can be seen from most of the garden. Others, such as the castellated Gothick Alcove, are tucked away in a small wood awaiting the pleasure of discovery.

Bishop Richard Pococke, an inveterate eighteenth-century traveler who documented his expeditions to country houses and parks in a manuscript entitled *Travels Through England,* was the first recorded visitor to the garden, in 1757. He wrote: "we came to Painswick, a market town prettily situated and on the side of a hill, and esteem'd an exceeding good air: just above it Mr. Hyett built an house of hewn stone, in a fine situation, and made a very pretty garden . . . the garden is on an hanging ground from the house in the vale . . . cut into walks through wood and adorn'd with water and buildings."[11]

Painswick's present owners, Lord and Lady Dickinson, who trace their ancestry back to the original owners, started the formidable task of restoring their unique garden in 1984. They were aided by an intricately detailed garden painting by Thomas Robins, commissioned in 1748 by Benjamin Hyett, son of the original owner and the one responsible for constructing Painswick's lovely garden. Robins's delightful watercolor, with its whimsical border of painted shells, butterflies, and flowers, was especially helpful in documenting the physical appearance as well as the placement of each garden building. It is quite possible that Robins may have executed the painting as a design guide to the grounds rather than as a record after its completion. It was one of five views of Hyett's properties Robins executed.

Painswick's beautiful garden is now close to its original appearance after considerable dredging, bulldozing, draining, replanting, and rebuilding. This tranquil setting is open to the public from February to mid-December.

This Gothick alcove, one of several follies at Painswick Rococo Garden in Gloucestershire, is approached by a path originally lined with beech trees; behind it one catches glimpses of the fertile Stroud Valley below.

Below: The restored Eagle House, prettily decked out with a pink stucco façade, is built into the side of an embankment. A pointed archway, flanked by a pair of niches, is crowned by castellation and a small hexagonal Gothick temple duplicating the one in Robins's painting (right).

Right: Thomas Robins was commissioned in 1748 to paint an overview of the Painswick gardens and this charming Gothick Eagle House, restored in 1991.

Exton Park

FORT HENRY AND DOVECOTE

Right: Fort Henry embodies Gothick fantasy at its best. Of Gloucester stone, it is edged in crenellation and detailed with overscale openwork pinnacles, a decorative door, and ogee windows.

Opposite: Swans glide among water lilies on the ornamental lake bordering Fort Henry, a wonderfully whimsical rococo Gothick summer house at Exton Park. Flanking the central room are two smaller rooms, one an entrance hall, and the other unfinished. Below, at water level, is a boathouse.

EXTON PARK is a large estate bordering a diminutive picture-book village composed of thatch-roofed cottages fronted by flowering gardens. Originally a deer park and woodland, now many of its acres are farmed. A number of wonderful follies are sprinkled about the grounds; the most magical is Fort Henry, about two miles to the east of the manor house. A wonderfully romantic Gothick summer house, recently restored after a fire all but destroyed it, Fort Henry was named after the sixth Earl of Gainsborough, who was responsible for its construction and was rumored to have enacted battles in miniature on its adjoining lake, one of a series of small lakes fed by a stream flowing throughout the park.

First viewed from across the ornamental lake, the inviting scene is the ultimate romantic vision. A family of snow-white swans glides serenely in the distance, sharing the pond with an assortment of other wildlife, while the round, scalloped-edged leaves of water lilies interrupt its smooth surface. On the distant shore, a Gothick pavilion topped with oversized pinnacles and crenellation sits invitingly on the edge, reflected in the tranquil water.

From across the meadow, Fort Henry appears much smaller than when viewed from the lakeside. Built into the side of an embankment at water's edge, the lower walls of the boathouse that contain Fort Henry's first floor are hidden from view. The crenellated fortress-like side walls of the boathouse form a low three-sided stone wall that seems to embrace the summer house above it, on the second floor. Enormous finials are positioned at each of its end posts, reinforcing a sense of fantasy with their exaggerated scale. The lakeside pavilion is also dwarfed by the great sweeping branches of a giant pine, some dipping into the water's surface, on its far side. Barbara Jones, in her definitive 1953 book, *Follies and Grottoes,* states, "No gothick decoration anywhere at any time was better than this."[12]

Another of Exton Park's Gothick follies not far from the main hall is a lovely octagonal dovecote, which sits surrounded by sheep in a field on the bank of another of the small lakes. First built in the eighteenth century, the pinnacled Gothick charmer had an arcaded semicircular cattle shed added to its base in the early nineteenth century. Architectural features include a pedimented central entrance and, above, the illusion of windows.

Exton Park is still in the family of Lord Gainsborough and is not open to the public.

Left: When one approaches this capricious lakeside pavilion by land, it appears to be much more diminutive.

Opposite: Exton Park's octagonal dovecote, ornamented with obelisk-shaped pinnacles and wrapped by an arcaded sheep shelter, seems to be lifted from a bucolic landscape painting.

Opposite: Fort Henry's delicate plasterwork was recently redone from castings of decorative elements remaining after a fire. The entrance through a small anteroom lies beyond.

Soft shadings accentuate Fort Henry's beautifully proportioned interior, a confection of creamy moldings and fan vaulting. Nineteenth-century French Gothic chairs from Mallett's accompany a table set for a hunt luncheon. The lilac-patterned cloth and plates are from Colefax and Fowler.

Molding framing this door repeats the feather-like motif found above the mantel. A beautiful incised leaf pattern is tucked into the apex of the ogee-arched door. On either side of the wall are large quatrefoils. Classical acanthus leaves form a cornice around the room.

Part II
Cottages
&
Garden
Dwellings

S THE TREND toward landscape gardens grew, grounds surrounding English country houses became dotted with a vast array of follies. The renowned gardens of Stowe alone contained forty-eight such structures. Follies assumed many forms, ranging from simple columns and arches to a rustic vine-covered cottage or a shell grotto complete with resident hermit.

The motivation for their construction varied as greatly as the forms they took. There were memorials to battle heroes and monarchs, tributes to wives or to a lost love—one tower was rumored to have been built as a reminder to an unfaithful wife; a few were erected for practical purposes, providing employment for hungry villagers, and some served as gatehouses, gamekeeper lodges, dairies, ice houses, cattle sheds, aviaries, hound houses, and even privies. Others were constructed solely for the pure pleasure they evoked in the eye of the beholder, ornaments to embellish the landscape and to excite the imagination.

Leading architects experimented freely with the tiny garden structures. (The magnificent fan vaults of Arbury Hall's reception rooms are believed by some to have been tried out in miniature by Henry Keene in a small garden temple at Enville.) The one common link among these eccentric, appealing, whimsical buildings was that each was delightfully unique and extremely personal.

It was only a matter of time before Gothick influences spread beyond the boundaries of country estates to farms and laborers' cottages, small humble dwellings scattered in fields and along the edges of roads or clustered together around central greens in village settings. The use of ornamentation here was quite arbitrary. Gothick windows and doorways, label moldings over casement windows, crocketed panels, and cusped windows—perhaps seen in a pattern book—brought an element of charm to vernacular cottages throughout the English countryside.

Cottages were not to remain the domain of the poor. Toward the end of the eighteenth century, as a fondness for nature and things rustic grew, and as the expanding Industrial Revolution fueled a desire to return to a simpler life, the concept of a rose-covered cottage was particularly appealing to many of the growing number of well-off middle-class English. Architects were quick to pick up on this burgeoning interest in country retreats, referred to as *cottages ornés*. Pattern books such as William F. Pocock's *Architectural Designs for Rustic Cottages and Picturesque Dwellings,* first introduced in the 1770s, offered the gentry a wide selection of picturesque cottage styles to select from, and Gothick was well represented.

John Papworth, in his 1818 pattern book, *Designs for Rural Residences,* wrote, "The cottage orné is a

new species of building in the economy of domestic architecture, and subject to its own laws of fitness and propriety. It is not the habitation of the laborious, but of the affluent, of the man of study, of science, or of leisure; it is often the rallying point of domestic comfort, and in this age of elegant refinement, a mere cottage would be incongruous with the nature of its occupancy."[1]

Earlier mid-eighteenth-century pattern books, such as those by Batty Langley, Paul Decker, and Thomas Lightolier, consisted of simple engravings silhouetted on the page. Those published later in the century and into the next by the likes of John B. Papworth, P. F. Robinson, Francis Goodwin, and John Plaw, using a new printing technique called aquatint, featured cottages and villas set in the midst of pretty gardens with distant rolling hills frequently thrown in for good measure. The relationship of the house to its setting reflected the strong influence of the Picturesque Movement and the importance it placed on landscaping. By the end of the century, architects like Humphrey Repton were designing Gothick cottages with high gables, decorative vergeboards, diamond-paned windows, and fanciful towering chimneys. Repton, a prominent landscape gardener, wrote, "The picturesque and pleasing effort of smoke ascending, when relieved by a dark hanging wood . . . , is a circumstance by no means to be neglected,"[2] a sentiment as well as a

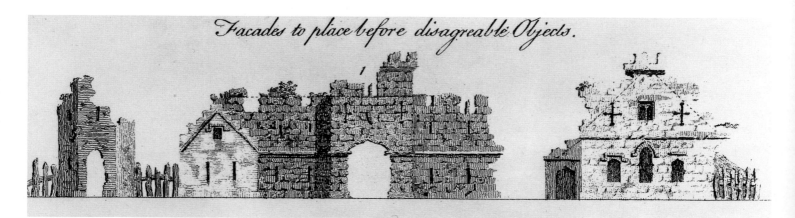

Facades to place before disagreable Objects.

style borrowed by nineteenth-century Americans Andrew Jackson Downing and Alexander Jackson Davis. Lord Chesterfield tagged these houses "Carpenter's Gothic." Architectural pattern books flourished until the arrival of the Victorian Age, which heralded the end of the Picturesque Movement.

The word "picturesque" was a familiar one commonly used by citizens of the late eighteenth century. In 1756 Edmund Burke attempted to classify the visual sensations by which man understands his world in a philosophical essay entitled "The Sublime and the Beautiful," establishing attributes for each that explain all aesthetic pleasure. The Reverend William Gilpin, a schoolmaster and travel writer who enjoyed painting pastoral views while on his many journeys, felt Burke missed a number of characteristics related to painting, adding "picturesque beauty" to the list. The term was further clarified in Uvedale Price's 1794 "An Essay on the Picturesque," when he assigned to it attributes such as roughness, irregularity of form, and interest in light and shadow, all elements easily translated into architecture.

During the eighteenth and early nineteenth centuries, landowners, in their zeal to create the picture-perfect romantic landscape garden, swept away existing villages housing their workers and replaced them with an assemblage of picturesque cottages. These pastoral villages incorporated into

Thomas Lightolier included several suggestions for "Facades to place before disagreeable Objects" in his 1762 publication, The Gentleman and Farmer's Architect . . . Containing a Great Variety of Useful and Genteel Designs. *Designed as Gothick sham ruins, they were intended to camouflage privies.*

estate parks were positioned to be seen from the manor house. Author James Chambers, in his informative book *The English House,* comments that "a number of landlords built Picturesque cottages and villages for their labourers, if for no other reason than to improve the approaches to their mansions. Many were inevitably Gothic."[3] Some landowners went so far as to insist that cottage dwellers dress up in long flowing robes or shepherd's costumes for effect.

The building of workers' cottages was not confined to private estates. Industrial concerns financed model villages to house workers and their families, motivated in large part by the desire to provide better living conditions for them. One of the most famous of the English model villages was Blaise Hamlet in Avon, designed by John Nash in 1810 at the request of banker John Scandrett Harford. This trend-setting village consisted of nine cottages grouped around a village green. Unlike earlier villages, where cookie-cutter cottages lined up in an orderly fashion, Blaise Hamlet simulated the natural evolution of a village, with cottages in different architectural styles positioned in irregular spots. One element all had in common was an elaborate ornamental chimney reminiscent of the exuberant chimneys dating back to Tudor times. During the nineteenth century, the influence of the romantic English Gothick cottage extended across the Atlantic; adapted to American needs, it became part of the fabric of American architecture.

Much of Gothick's appeal was fueled by literary endeavors that were the product of the Romantic Movement. Among the luminaries who were particularly instrumental in fostering a taste for Gothick were a handful of poets and writers who shared an interest in archaeology. The most distinguished of the group was Thomas Gray, a poet and a scholar of medieval literature and architecture who, as a traveling companion of Horace Walpole's, is believed to have had an influence on Walpole's selection of the Gothick style for his country house. Another was Thomas Wharton, an archaeologist who wrote an influential essay in 1762 encouraging the use of Gothick.

In addition, romantic poets and writers such as Blake, Wordsworth, Byron, and Coleridge glorified what they saw as the victory of the senses over the intellect, expressing in their works a love of nature and the simple life. The immensely popular 1798 publication of *Lyrical Ballads* by Wordsworth and Coleridge, which praised unrestrained nature as a force that liberated man's imagination, heralded Romanticism's overwhelming acceptance.

Gothic novels and historic romances popular during the second half of the eighteenth and into the nineteenth centuries exuded a fascination for the melancholy and the sentimental. In 1764 Horace Walpole wrote *The Castle of Otranto,* the first of the so-called Gothic novels. Set in medieval times in an Italian castle evocative of Walpole's own English country house, it was full of melancholy, young love, and the supernatural. In its first edition Walpole actually claimed that it had been reprinted from a recently discovered medieval manuscript.

Charles Eastlake recognized Walpole's *Castle of Otranto* as "the first modern work of fiction which depended for its interest on the incidents of a chivalrous age, and it thus became the prototype of that class of novel which was afterwards imitated by Mrs. Ratcliffe and perfected by Sir Walter Scott."[4] Numerous books written in the same vein shortly followed suit. Rich in sentiment but light on historic research, they all contained heroic larger-than-life figures and expressed the darker side of Gothick's fascination with the mysterious and the supernatural. Mary Shelley, wife of the poet, was to take Gothic literature into a new direction, writing

Frankenstein when she was nineteen. Many recognize her as the first science-fiction writer with the publication of this 1817 thriller.

Gothick's hold on the literary imagination was also advanced by the work of Sir Walter Scott, who brought another dimension to Gothic literature. Under his substantial influence, which reached across to America and the Continent, Gothic fiction strayed from tales of horror to simple melodramas with characters that were more true-to-life. His vivid descriptions of medieval times were invaluable in spreading the Gothic style. Kenneth Clark, in his 1928 book *The Gothic Revival,* commented that "it is the wealth of archaeological detail in Scott's novels which made his picture of the Middle Ages so satisfying and so much more influential than the mere melancholy of the poets."[5] The most famous historical novel of the age was Scott's *Ivanhoe: A Romance,* an adventure story of medieval chivalry published in 1820.

Painters of the time, far from immune to the lure of nature, captured the prevailing spirit of the Gothic movement on canvas. Important English landscape painters John Constable and J. M. W. Turner best expressed the romantic notion of landscape. Constable's tranquil scenes encapsulated the rural ideal, with gentle cultivated fields, calm streams with cottages nestled on their banks, and, in the distance, a church spire.

The desire to escape to a tranquil country retreat is as appealing today as it was two centuries ago, when a growing English middle class, the product of a population that had almost doubled between the beginning and end of the eighteenth century, found a special appeal in a rustic rural cottage. The cottage orné, based on a stylish, sophisticated model of the simple life, became among the most fashionable expressions of the Picturesque Movement, finding favor with not only the middle class but with the wealthy as well.

This "Villa in the Cottage Style" is one of thirty-eight engravings from a 1795 publication by John Plaw entitled Ferme Ornée; or, Rural Improvements . . . . All are sepia-colored and engraved in "aqua-tinta," a process that provided subtle shadings and gave the effect of a wash drawing.

Villa in the Cottage Stile.

An 1815 advertisement of Houghton Lodge in The Statesman reads, "The cottage has been erected within a few years at very great expense, and finished in a very superior and chaste style with Gothic embellishments, affording accommodation for a family of the first respectability." [6]

Houghton Lodge

Above: The lovely Peacock Garden is entered through an iron gate ornamented with Gothic motifs.

HOUGHTON LODGE, set in a tranquil spot near Stockbridge in Hampshire, is the ultimate picturesque cottage. Once past a Gothick entrance gate and charming twin gatehouses, visitors can catch a glimpse of the lodge at the end of a wide drive lined with towering beech trees that dwarf the handsome cottage. Built around 1800 as a gentlemen's retreat or fishing lodge on about fifty acres, Houghton is believed by some to be designed by architect John Plaw, who was responsible for a number of neighboring structures. The lodge is similar to one of the plates in Plaw's 1795 publication, *Ferme Ornée; or, Rural Improvements . . . Calculated for Landscape and Picturesque Effects.*

A pair of large quatrefoil windows gracing the façade first capture the

The picturesque mirror-image Gothick gatehouses announcing the entrance to Houghton Lodge, an enchanting cottage orné in Hampshire, are trimmed with decorative vergeboards, large quatrefoils, and extended chimneys.

visitor's attention. Most of the lodge's windows, however, face away from the drive to a great expanse of open lawn that slopes gently down to the River Test. Little more than a stream, the river, celebrated for its trout fishing, meanders by at a leisurely pace. Just beyond it, a pleasant pastoral scene stretches out across the flat landscape, complete with cows grazing peacefully in a neighboring meadow. In the spring, fields of daffodils streak the drive and riverbank with gold.

Houghton Lodge's early history is vague. It is believed to have been built by a Mr. Bernard. The cottage, with its six second-floor bedrooms and dressing rooms, was advertised for sale locally in 1800 shortly after it was constructed, most probably because of the death of its owner, and again the following January in the *Times*. Fourteen years

The veranda looks across a gently sloping lawn to the tranquil River Test. Built in 1860 of wrought iron, the frame is believed to have originally been constructed of twigs.

A hedge decoratively trimmed with whimsical topiary in the form of birds delineates the Peacock Garden, a recently redesigned knot garden on the spacious grounds. The knot was a geometric pattern within a square, made of box and herbs clipped into shape. It was developed in medieval times.

later the house and grounds were on the market once more.

Houghton Lodge is a wonderful storybook example of a cottage orné, with a deep hipped roof that rounds out into a large dome to the back of the cottage, and clusters of decorated molded brick chimneys soaring high above the roofline. Originally thatched, its roof was replaced in the nineteenth century by tile. On the south side, small, steeply pitched dormered windows with scalloped decorative trim extend from the roof. Below them, the pointed windows of the drawing room dip to the floor and open out to a small court.

The cottage was symmetrical, until a small addition of stables was built around 1808 to house fourteen horses and three coaches. This was later converted to a smoking room and kitchen, which was moved from its original location in the basement. A circular music room overlooking the river protrudes on the east side, creating a large bow. Just beyond it is a Victorian veranda that may have replaced an original rustic one constructed of twigs; built in 1860 of cast iron, its scroll work is typical of the period. The dining room to the right of the music room has a window framed in pewter, its design reflecting an Indian influence.

Houghton Lodge is now the property of Captain and Mrs. Busk, who inherited it in 1980 and are in the process of restoring it. The cottage and its surrounding grounds have passed down through Mrs. Busk's family, going to the youngest daughter. Overnight guests are welcomed occasionally and a tour of the interior and the garden can be arranged.

Clytha Castle

Above: This hilltop folly castle, straight out of the pages of a child's storybook, lies in the heart of Wales. Designed with Gothick windows, quatrefoils, and crenellation along its roofline, its two round towers are hollow.

Opposite: A view of Clytha Castle's square tower. The folly includes living quarters and is available for holiday rentals through the Landmark Trust.

ONE OF THE MOST lyrical of follies is to be found in Wales. Built in the guise of a small castle, this fanciful masquerade, purported to be the work of architect John Nash, was constructed as a touching memorial. An eloquent plaque centered on the front of Clytha Castle reads: "Erected in the year 1790 by William Jones of Clytha House, husband of Elizabeth, last surviving child of Sir William Morgan of Tredegar, it was undertaken with the purpose of relieving a mind afflicted by the loss of a most excellent wife, to the memory of whose virtues this tablet is dedicated." Gwyn Headley and Wim Meulencamp captured the essence of this magical place when they wrote in 1986: "Jones found solace in stone. The building he left us is pure magic; derivative yet wildly original, it is a late

This Building was erected in the Year 1790 by
WILLIAM JONES of Clytha House Esq.
Fourth Son of JOHN JONES
of Lanarth Court Monmouthshire Esq. and
Husband of ELIZABETH the last surviving Child
of Sir WILLIAM MORGAN of Tredegar K·B
and Grand-Daughter of the most Noble WILLIAM
second Duke of Devonshire
It was undertaken for the purpose of relieving a mind
sincerely afflicted by the loss of a most excellent Wife
whose Remains were deposited
in Lanarth Church Yard A·D: 1787
and to the Memory of whose Virtues
this Tablet is dedicated.

Clytha Castle was built to ease its owner's mind at the loss of his beloved wife. This plaque set in the center of the folly relates the touching story.

The main estate, which can be glimpsed from the tiny castle in the valley below, has at its entrance a Gothick archway trimmed with crockets and pinnacles. A small Gothick gatehouse adjoins it.

Clytha Castle's square tower, the pivotal point in this L-shaped folly, includes several rooms that extend behind a screen running across the ornamental front.

fling of Strawberry Hill Gothick, to a pattern which is its own master."[7]

The castle sits picturesquely on the summit of a hill, half-hidden in a grove of ancient chestnuts and encircled by a ha-ha. In front of it, a charming pastoral scene spreads out across the landscape, with rolling manicured fields populated by grazing cows and sheep. Positioned to be seen from Clytha House in the valley below, it was originally used by the family as a retreat, for picnics, or simply as an excuse for a long leisurely walk. More recently, the castle was home to the estate gamekeeper.

Its unusual L-shaped form sports three towers, the end two round and the central one square, joined by two curtain walls. The most distinctive and unusual feature of the castle is its north curtain wall, which sweeps up to a crown-like pinnacle. Large crenellations run around the towers and walls. Decorative quatrefoils, trefoils, lancet windows, arrow slits (narrow openings through which arrows were shot), and crosses, all reminiscent of its medieval inspiration, are utilized as ornamentation all over its lovely pink stucco façade.

The round tower to the east is open to the air, as is the top of the back tower to the west, whose first floor houses a round bedroom. The square south tower in the middle has two rooms, each with ceilings about twenty feet high. The upper room, once resplendent with delicate plasterwork, is connected to the lower by a spiral staircase and was used as a chapel in the nineteenth century.

This once-loved folly stood empty and neglected for twenty-five years until the Landmark Trust, a charity that rescues historic buildings from vandalism and demolition, recently took a long lease on Clytha Castle and repaired the beguiling structure. Now furnished, it is available for holiday rentals through the Trust.

Frampton Court
Orangery

THE LYRICAL FRAMPTON COURT orangery is Gothick at its most successful. It is located on the east bank of the River Severn in Frampton-on-Severn, Gloucestershire, one of the prettiest villages in the Severn Vale, with its charming collection of half-timbered houses and thatched cottages surrounded by beautiful countryside.

The fanciful Gothick pavilion built in 1752 is an early example of the follies that began adorning landscape gardens of the eighteenth century. About three hundred yards north of its classical manor house, the fanciful wedding-cake-looking garden pavilion is mirrored in the still water of a decorative canal stretching out two hundred yards. The ornamental carp-

filled Dutch canal curves midway along its east side, which is bordered by flowering shrubs, roses, and herbaceous plants.

The fragrance of fruit trees was appealing to the romantically inclined eighteenth-century landowners, leading a number of them to construct buildings to house a wide assortment of tropical trees. The ground floor of the orangery was set up as a greenhouse for plants and flowers and probably housed a variety of flowering fruit trees as well.

The orangery is composed of two octagons unit-

ed by a rectangular hall with a cantilevered stone staircase to the rear, which winds its way up a third octagonal tower. Crowned by a cupola, the parapet of the third tower is decked out with battlements and pinnacles. The beautiful hexagonal glazing bars of the ogee arched windows and doors, typical of the early Gothick motifs, reinforce the folly's faceted surface and add a decorative touch to the confection. The ogee arch, featured prominently in Batty Langley's publication *Gothic Architecture Improved,* was believed to have originated in the Near

Opposite: An ogee-arched doorway, a form repeated throughout the folly, frames the graceful cantilevered stone stairway situated in the orangery's back octagonal tower.

This tile-lined stone fireplace in the dining room, one of two in the building, was originally upstairs in a room used to take tea or possibly to paint. The ogee curve outlining its top and opening echoes the Gothick arches of the folly's windows and doors.

East in the fourteenth century and was introduced as a decorative element in the Gothic Decorated period around the same time. Interest in the "exotic" in the eighteenth century brought together a mix of cultural influences, such as this motif.

While the designer of the pavilion is not known, the lively folly has the appearance of a scaled-down version of Stout's Hill, a manor house also situated in Gloucestershire that was designed by William Halfpenny and closely resembles designs found in his and his brother John's 1752 pattern book, *Chinese and Gothic Architecture Properly Ornamented.*

The second floor of the orangery was probably used for afternoon tea and possibly the pursuit of creative endeavors, such as painting. Its interior contains two decorative Gothick fireplaces that initially were upstairs but now are on the ground floor, which was converted from a conservatory to the drawing room and dining rooms. Recently restored by its present owners, the Cliffords—a family who can trace its roots back to the twelfth-century Old Manor located across the village green from Frampton Court—the delightful Gothick orangery is now available for holiday rentals.

The Ring

Above: The tiny arched rustic entrance to the little Hansel-and-Gretel cottage is patterned with twigs and edged with gingerbread carving. It is joined at its peak by a simple finial.

Opposite: Tucked away in a woodland, this enchanting cottage was built in 1776 as an aviary on the grounds of a vast country estate. The Ring is now a weekend retreat, where wild pheasant roam the grounds and pale roses climb the walls and roof.

BESTIARIES, or menageries, as the French referred to them, were very much in vogue in the eighteenth century. During this time all manner of beasts inhabited the grounds of English country estates, from common livestock to the more wild of the animal kingdom, such as lions, tigers, polar bears, and kangaroos, joined by an assortment of exotic birds from storks to peacocks. Often the structures housing them were Gothick in design.

Just such a building was included on the grounds of one of the largest of the English country houses located not far from London. Here, a picturesque Gothick aviary built in 1776 to shelter exotic Indian pheasant was positioned on a hillside some distance from the main house and christened The Ring because of its construction on the remains of an ancient Saxon fort. Like many follies scattered throughout the grounds of country estates, it had been long neglected and ravaged by time.

This diminutive aviary was luckier than most, however. Betty Hanley, an American woman who makes her home in London, came upon it in 1973 while visiting friends for the weekend who lived nearby. It had been a rainy Saturday and they decided to go exploring. Unable to resist the rustic cottage when she glimpsed it half-hidden in a tangle of undergrowth and trees, Ms. Hanley set about to buy or lease the crumbling cottage, which at this point was marked for demolition. The task proved to be an arduous one, for Ms. Hanley had quite a fight convincing the owner to lease the dilapidated structure to her. Ultimately, her persistence finally won him over.

While her considerable creative powers gave her the ability to envision what the ruin might become, Ms. Hanley was not fully prepared for what such a restoration would entail. The cottage had originally been built of lath and plaster by the same man who constructed a rococo Gothick chapel on the estate grounds. When the new owner took the cottage over, trees were growing out of its roof. Undaunted, she worked diligently to restore only what was absolutely necessary. The roof had to be raised three feet, a wall constructed where it was originally open to allow access for the birds and water, and electricity installed. Reconstruction took over a year.

Ms. Hanley decorated the interior in an eclectic manner, mixing Gothick elements, such as the arches framing her drawing-room bookcases, with her other possessions. In the lovely dining room, with its trompe l'œil paneling, the Gothick fireplace and chairs are copies from the chapel. The dining room is dominated by three floor-to-ceiling

Gothick windows opening to a small veranda and garden just beyond filled with flowering cherry trees. Furnished with taste and imagination, the Gothick cottage captures the comfort and warmth exemplified in the best of English country houses.

Above: The drawing room sports pointed bookcases flanking the fireplace. A Gothick chair sits at the desk.

Opposite: The cottage entry doubles as a dining room. Its walls are striated to create the illusion of paneling. A large round dining table is surrounded by painted Gothick chairs, copied from ones in a nearby chapel. Three large Gothick windows look out to a garden filled with cherry trees.

Inwardleigh Cottage

Above: This cottage in a southern English hamlet started life at about half its present size, topped with a thatched roof. It is now the country home of decorator Bridget Glasgow and her husband, David.

Opposite: Gothick diamond-paned windows bring a touch of whimsy to the front of the cottage and set the style for its charming interior.

AN EIGHTEENTH-CENTURY COTTAGE, one of a handful bordering a narrow country lane in a sleepy hamlet in southwestern England, is home to talented decorator Bridget Glasgow and her husband. It was the Gothick windows of this simple cottage that first attracted Ms. Glasgow's attention. The couple initially rented it, when told the cottage was not for sale, and eventually convinced the owner to sell it to them.

Ms. Glasgow had started her own design business in nearby Salisbury after working in London for a number of years at the prestigious design firm of Colefax and Fowler. (Much of the fabric used throughout the cottage is from that firm.) It took four years to remodel the cottage, as the

new owners extended it to include an ample drawing room with a conservatory off the back overlooking a pleasant garden. The small 1730 cottage originally had a somewhat lopsided look, but is now symmetrical with its recent addition.

Inside, the cottage projects an air of warmth and comfort; its welcoming entrance hall, the oldest part of the house, sets the tone for the rest of the cottage. A large stone fireplace, with its original bread oven to one side, dominates the small room. A desk is positioned next to the window. Walls are covered in a subtle stripe and windows are draped in a strawberry toile, their arched pelmets repeat-

Above: The front entrance, just to the left of the window, opens into this comfortable study with its ample fireplace, a favorite spot on cold winter days.

Below: A large eighteenth-century Swedish chest is right at home in the English cottage's small dining room. Pointed upholstered side chairs repeat the window's silhouette.

ing the shape of the Gothick windows. A loveseat covered in the same pattern gives a cohesiveness to the cozy room, a favorite spot in the winter when accompanied by a roaring fire. The owner's fondness for strawberries is reflected throughout her cottage.

Pointed backs of upholstered dining room chairs reiterate the Gothick theme. Walls covered in a pale peach damask wallpaper bring a warm glow to the room. Tableware is stored in a nineteenth-century Swedish sideboard painted robin's-egg blue. The crewel fabric of the dining-room curtains and the sisal carpeting used throughout help retain a casual look.

The inviting new drawing room hides its secret

Above: The graceful curving valance at the front window in the drawing room, the most recent addition to the cottage, follows the shape of the Gothick window. The pointed side chair flanking it reinforces the Gothick theme.

Reds and blues were selected for Inwardleigh Cottage's drawing room, a decidedly stylish yet relaxed country room. The side door leads to a lovely back garden.

well, appearing as though it were always part of the cottage. The Gothick motif is carried into the room, with pointed bookcases flanking a stone fireplace. The pelmets topping the windows and the door leading to the plant-filled conservatory and garden beyond are gently arched. The same pattern as in the draperies covers a sofa, complemented by checks and stripes on a loveseat and chairs.

A concern for detail, from a subtle wallpaper border or narrow braid edging walls, to contrast binding on upholstery and window treatments, combined with an unerring sense of style, have created a highly personal country home that reflects its owners' tastes—a home that will surely bring them pleasure for many years to come.

Above: Narrow stairs in the quaint cottage, illuminated with light from the pointed diamond-paned window at the top of the landing, lead to several bedrooms on the second floor.

Right: A decorative red woven tape trims the walls of the master bedroom as well as the pointed scallops of the bed canopy and shades.

Opposite: The use of a rosy toile fabric for the walls, drapery, and dust ruffle creates a cozy atmosphere in the cottage's small guest bedroom.

Chandos Lodge

Opposite: Once you step inside the garden gates of Chandos Lodge, the hustle-bustle of the small village just outside its walls is lost and the magic of the house and its gardens takes possession.

Above: This charming lodge has undergone a number of changes since its 1810 construction. One of the more recent is this Gothick conservatory added at the rear.

CHANDOS LODGE, hidden behind a sturdy brick wall encircling its eight-acre estate, is actually only a few blocks from the center of a simple English village. Painted a soft clear pink, like numerous houses that dot the surrounding spare landscape, the charming villa is distinguished by a set of Gothick windows that look out onto an expanse of lawn punctuated by a reflecting pond and topiary garden.

The lodge was originally built in 1810 by Thomas Wythe, who christened it Chandos in honor of a likely love interest, the widow of Henry Bridges, the second Duke of Chandos. In more recent times, Chandos Lodge became the cherished country retreat of world-famous choreogra-

Opposite: The pink of the façade has been repeated inside in this sunny dining room, one of the original sections of the lodge. A delicate Gothick cornice adds a touch of confection. The nineteenth-century cast-iron heater to the left has been electrified.

Right: A central cantilevered staircase is situated at one end of the dining room. Beyond is a small morning room that, like the dining room, is original to the house.

pher Sir Frederick Ashton, who acquired the house and its grounds shortly before he was knighted in 1962. The romantic structure is just the sort one would expect to appeal to the imaginative Ashton, who until his death at eighty-three in 1988 frequently returned to Chandos, finding in the quiet spot not only an escape from his demanding life but a source of inspiration as well.

By the time Ashton assumed possession, the lodge had doubled in size. Toward the end of the nineteenth century, additional rooms were constructed on both ends of the original central portion. The area to the west was utilized as a storage room, with its entrance through the kitchen, but when it was later converted into a sitting room its access was changed, so that it opened onto the

dining room. Sir Fred, as he was affectionately called by friends, continued the Gothick tradition, installing a beautiful Gothick window and door, most probably originally part of a church, to the rear of this room. He also added Gothick moldings to the dining room and the morning room, both of which feature the original Gothick windows. Most of the pottery throughout the house is inexpensive, having been collected by Ashton while poking through antique shops with friends when they came to visit.

Ashton made a number of changes throughout the grounds, adding a topiary garden and a pond mirroring the lodge, their construction funded by profits from his choreography for the film *The Tales of Beatrix Potter,* made in 1971. Ashton also built a

small Gothick conservatory behind the lodge that overlooks a garden and what was once the stables.

Ashton, whom many credit with the development of a distinctly British ballet style, was known for his versatility and his classical bent, choreographing the first of more than fifty ballets in 1926. In 1963 he became director of the Royal Ballet. When he first joined the troupe in 1935 it was called the Vics-Wells, later becoming the Sadler's Wells Ballet. Ashton worked closely with the famed ballerina Dame Margot Fonteyn, who described him as the greatest choreographer of our time. Upon Ashton's death, his nephew inherited Chandos Lodge. Now, with recent restoration and the prized possessions of the new owner, the house stands ready to delight another generation.

Right: The comfortable morning room doubles as an entrance hall. Gothick molding, a small lantern, and the quatrefoil-patterned wallpaper from Cole, a copy of a nineteenth-century original, reinforce the Gothick theme.

Below: Chandos Lodge's front entrance was originally at the foot of the central staircase. Above it is a Gothick window and a small balcony now connecting one of the bedrooms to a bath. The Gothick chairs on the balcony are nineteenth-century.

Left: This sitting room, a late-nineteenth-century addition, was initially a storage area. Its Gothick door and window, flanked by pointed-arched cabinets rimmed with quatrefoils, were added by Sir Frederick Ashton.

Part III

Gothic Manor

Houses

of the

Eighteenth

Century

he eighteenth century was a time of relative stability in England; economic changes brought greater prosperity and, under Robert Walpole, England's first prime minister, a cabinet was set up that functioned as a central organ of government. The British Empire added India, Australia, New Zealand, and Canada to its fold, and, following the founding of the Bank of England in 1694, it dominated the world of trade and finance as well.

Aristocrats and the landed gentry, motivated by travels to ancient European cities or simply by the desire to outdo their neighbors, constructed magnificent new residences or restored structures built a century or two earlier. But, unlike much of the wealthy on the continent who chose to construct elaborate city residences along broad boulevards, the English, with their long-standing love for the country, elected instead to channel fortunes into the construction of country houses, most of which were set in the midst of expansive grounds.

Many of these houses, frequently financed by agricultural rents or mining, were specifically designed for entertaining on a grand scale in an era when friends often stayed on for weeks. They were not only proclamations of their owners' wealth, education, and taste but a major avenue to social recognition and political power. Fueled by the discovery of Pompeii and Herculaneum in 1748, the most popular architectural style for

these grand houses during much of the century was neoclassicism, governed by the precepts of restraint, balance, and unity. Gothick, during the early decades of the eighteenth century, was, for the most part, relegated to the garden. There were, however, scattered examples early in the 1700s of Gothic motifs that had been adopted for residences by architects such as Sir John Vanbrugh in his 1717 castle-like house at Greenwich. Jane Davies, in her introduction to the catalog for the 1976 Houston Museum of Fine Arts Gothic show, wrote: "In the late seventeenth and early eighteenth centuries Sir Christopher Wren and his followers on occasion used an approximation of Gothic, and Sir John Vanbrugh demonstrated a feeling for Gothic form, but it was in the second quarter of the eighteenth century that 'Rococo Gothick' had its beginning, when William Kent and Sanderson Miller introduced the use of Gothic details in a purely decorative manner, adapted and applied to classical forms."[1] While more often associated with the Palladian architecture popularized by his mentor, Lord Burlington, the multitalented William Kent was one of the first to explore the use of Gothick embellishments to evoke the past. Around 1730 Kent created a country house at Esher Place in Surrey for financier

Henry Pelham by joining two semi-octagonal towers of a late-fifteenth-century gatehouse and turning the carriageway between them into an entrance hall. Kent added ogee Gothick windows and large quatrefoil openings to the towers and the connecting unit.

The formation of the Antiquarian Society, which was started by gentlemen of taste and learning who were fascinated with the study of medieval life and culture, became a driving force in the revival of Gothic. By mid-century, encouraged by the enthusiastic Horace Walpole and other early advocates, the Gothick style finally found its way to English manor houses. The early 1750s proved to be a propitious time for the movement, with the Gothicizing of three outstanding manor houses—Strawberry Hill, Arbury Hall, and Alscot Park. Their owners—Horace Walpole, Roger Newdigate, and James West, respectively—were all committed antiquarians. Each managed to capture the Gothick spirit through the use of exuberant ornamentation only vaguely reminiscent of its medieval roots.

The house that catapulted Gothick into the public eye was Strawberry Hill, the intriguing creation of the oft-quoted literary lion Horace Walpole, who had acquired a taste for Gothic after embarking on the Grand Tour with friend and poet Thomas Gray, an ardent Gothic admirer. Picturesque and capricious, the asymmetrical Strawberry Hill was an intensely personal expression of the taste of its owner. The younger son of Sir Robert Walpole, the witty Horace had many social and political contacts that made him something of a fashion arbiter, and his selection of the unconventional Gothick gave it a healthy boost toward respectability.

Eighty miles to the north, another ambitious Gothick remodeling had begun in 1752. Grander in scale, the flamboyant additions at Arbury Hall,

Roger Newdigate's manor house, continued for fifty years. Its splendid interiors featured early Gothick at its best. Mary Ann Evans, better known as George Eliot, was born in 1819 on the Newdigate estate, where her father was steward. Growing up with stories of the Newdigate family, she used these and the physical characteristics of the house as material for several of her novels. Eliot described the intricate plasterwork of the saloon ceiling as "petrified lace-work picked out with delicate and varied coloring. . . . a grand Gothic canopy."[2]

Completing the trio, James West's Alscot Park, located in the picturesque Cotswolds, was considerably smaller than Arbury Hall. Its lovely interiors are filled with a delightful plasterwork pastiche that brings together classical elements with fanciful Georgian Gothick.

Throughout the remainder of the century, Gothick designs were adopted both by those who were captivated by its whimsical lighthearted rococo spirit and by the more antiquarian-minded, who found greater appeal in a closer accuracy to the style's medieval ancestry. But until the third decade of the nineteenth century, the use of Gothic motifs was basically decorative—appearance was the only thing that counted. Terence Davis aptly describes this early period in *The Gothick Taste,* focusing on Georgian Gothick: "the design and decoration of most Gothick houses was lighthearted, unrealistic and sometimes frivolous. Herein lies the magic—in these very qualities of improbability and escapism—and the further they are removed from these realms the less magical they become. This make-believe aspect is the strength and weakness of the Gothick taste."[3]

Exterior additions, from simple pointed windows and interlocking fanlight tracery to more elaborate turrets, battlements, crocketed finials, and bay windows, brought an animation to previously staid manor houses. Decorative interior alterations, usually limited to the library and the entrance hall, were playful and imaginative.

Mixing classical and Gothic as well as Chinese forms together in one structure was quite acceptable throughout the eighteenth century. Castleward, in County Down, Ireland, is an interesting example of this. In 1772 its owners, Lord and Lady Bangor, decided to update their sixteenth-century country house; Lady Bangor was set on using Gothic motifs, while her husband was just as determined that it should be redone in the popular Palladian style. The resolution was a compromise. The house's formal southwest façade is pedimented and colonnaded, while its northeast garden façade is decked out in Gothick splendor, with pointed windows and battlements. Inside, the saloon and sitting rooms are fancifully Gothick, in contrast to the classical restraint of the hall, dining room, and music room. Castleward, now the property of the National Trust and open to the public, and Moore Abbey in County Kildare, are the only surviving examples of major Irish manor houses in the Gothick style.

Toward the end of the eighteenth century, extremely large manor houses became fashionable, the largest being the mammoth Fonthill Abbey on Wilshire Downs, constructed in 1794 and designed by architect James Wyatt. The most incredible country house of its time, Fonthill seemed to spark the imagination of all of England. Built as a summer retreat for William Beckford, who inherited a vast fortune in Jamaican sugar plantations and slaves upon the death of his father, London's Lord Mayor, it was intended as a residential rival to the great cathedrals of the Middle Ages.

The cruciform-shaped structure was constructed initially of timber and cement by five hundred workmen who toiled day and night. Fonthill measured 312 feet north to south and 270 feet east to west, with eighteen bedrooms and a gallery that ran a length of 185 feet. The immense central 128-foot-high octagonal grand saloon was topped with a 276-foot-high tower. Visible for miles, it collapsed in 1799, but was rebuilt in time for a visit from Lord Nelson and Lady Hamilton. When Beckford decided to live at Fonthill Abbey full-time, he rebuilt the tower of stone, but again it came toppling down and demolished part of the house in 1819, shortly after the estate was sold. Little remains of the massive structure today.

Fonthill Abbey's gardens were planned on the prevailing Picturesque theory, which held that a building should share a symbiotic relationship with its surrounding grounds. During the first year alone, Beckford planted one million trees. Fonthill, however, was never really comfortable within its landscape because of its overwhelming size.

Wyatt, having gained invaluable experience earlier in the restoration of medieval Gothic cathedrals, was instrumental in establishing a taste for Gothick by the turn of the century. Yet, Terence Davis writes, "although Wyatt's grasp of Gothic techniques was masterly . . . they were . . . no more authentic."[4] He undertook at least ten grand manor houses in the last fifteen years of his life, but Ashridge, in Hertfordshire, designed by Wyatt in 1807 and carried out by his nephew Jeffry Wyattville after Wyatt's unfortunate death in a coach accident, is the only one that has survived.

During the mid-eighteenth century, a brief flirtation with ornamental Gothic elements descended upon typical Georgian furniture forms. Like Batty Langley's imaginative architectural flights of fancy, they bore little resemblance to original historical styles. A limited amount of genuine medieval furniture existed, and in the interim a plethora of new forms had come into existence. Consequently, architects and cabinetmakers borrowed architectural

A pair of beautiful English Gothick chairs, dated circa 1820, are designed in the manner of George Smith or James Wyatt. Painted in gray-white and outlined in gold, their seats are caned.

motifs from medieval cathedrals for furniture, freely incorporating carved pinnacles, pointed arches, tracery, quatrefoils, crestings, crockets, and crenellations into chairs, cabinets, tables, bookcases, and the like. The only structural—as opposed to decorative—Gothic form adopted in furniture design was the clustered column, which was utilized for legs of tables and, occasionally, chairs. Even the ubiquitous English Windsor chair, normally found in a country-house library, became gothicized, sporting a pointed back and three pierced splats inspired by window tracery.

English furniture design books were latecomers on the scene, first appearing in the second quarter of the eighteenth century, because little importance was placed on furniture in the sparely furnished grand English houses of the seventeenth century.

The first pattern book to feature Gothick furniture for interiors was Mathew Darly's *A New Book of Chinese, Gothic & Modern Chairs*, issued in 1751. Darly, a talented engraver, also worked on the illustrations for Thomas Chippendale's highly successful *The Gentleman & Cabinet-Maker's Director*, first published in 1754. A number of respected furniture designers of the day, such as George Hepplewhite and Robert Adam, turned for a short time to Gothick motifs when it was considered trendy.

Pattern books were important because they functioned as sales catalogues for furniture designers such as Chippendale, an astute businessman as well as a designer, whose polished design book attracted wealthy clients to his cabinetmaking shop. The first edition of his beautifully illustrated *Director* reflected current trends, with an emphasis on the more

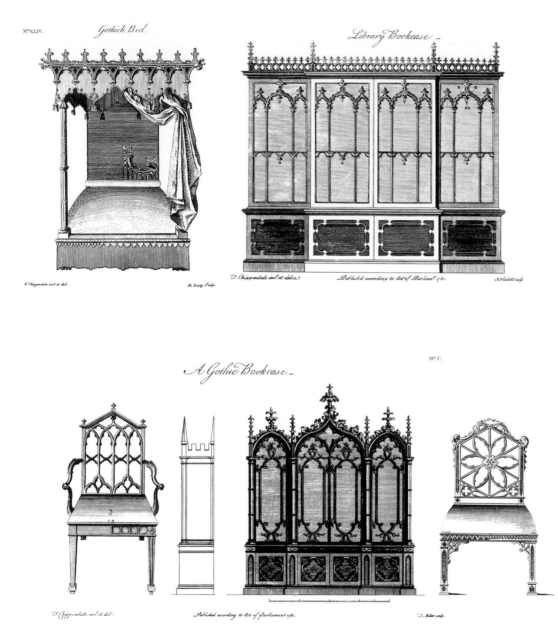

N.°XLIV.   *Gothich Bed.*

Library Bookcase.

A Gothic Bookcase.   N.° C.

Left: During the
mid-eighteenth century, a
number of leading cabinetmakers, such as Thomas
Chippendale, incorporated
fanciful Gothick elements into
their designs. Those shown
here are from the third edition
of Chippendale's The
Gentleman & Cabinet-
Maker's Director,
published in 1754.

Opposite: The publication
of measured engravings of
original Gothic structures,
such as these from Augustus
Pugin's Examples
of Gothic Architecture,
was particularly helpful to
architects interested in
experimenting with Gothic.
Shown here are details of a
canopy and base of a niche from
the west front of the gateway at
Magdalene College, Oxford,
dated 1829, and an oriel
window dated 1828 from
Balliol College, Oxford.

exotic and playful, incorporating elements of Gothick, chinoiserie, and rococo. Two editions followed;
of the 162 designs in the third edition, a dozen were
whimsical fantasized versions of Gothick.

As in architecture, a number of furniture pattern
books featured Gothick and Chinese designs combined in one piece of furniture. Few people at the

time recognized the difference between the two
styles, grouping them together simply as elements
of the flamboyant and exotic rococo style brought
over from France in the 1740s. Both shared sinuous
linear curves. Chinoiserie, the eighteenth-century
English vision of Chinese style, like Gothick, usually strayed far from its original origins, as designers

freely lifted motifs from exported porcelains, wallpaper, and other Oriental goods, creating fanciful designs with little basis in historic tradition.

The absence of books with engravings and measured details from original Gothic designs, such as those by the extraordinarily talented sixteenth-century architect Andrea Palladio, which had been a major aid in fostering classical influences in architecture, had slowed the spread of Gothick; however, after 1790, John Carter, Augustus Pugin, and John Britton published a number of illustrated books on medieval antiquities that were especially helpful for early-nineteenth-century architects experimenting with Gothic forms. Even the revered classicalist Sir John Soane tried his hand at Gothick

in the library at Stowe, Buckinghamshire, in 1805.

Gothick had finally arrived. Although many at the time were ready to write Gothick off as nothing but a passing fad, it persisted, inspiring respected architects, men of learning, and those in assorted artistic fields. While the eccentric style was diametrically opposed to the decidedly formal forms of classicism in the forefront of fashion, the conflict between the two styles was to produce an intriguing tension that became an important element in Gothick's appeal.

After 1830, serious, carefully researched adaptations were to bring a respectability to the Gothick style when, adopted by the Victorians, it ultimately evolved into a movement of gigantic proportions.

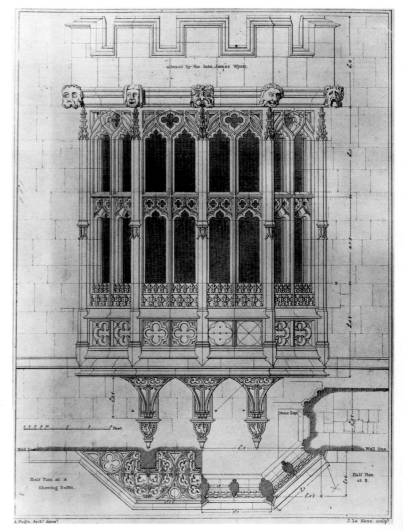

St. Michael's Mount

CORNWALL possesses a character distinctly its own. A region rich in prehistoric remains dating back to the Iron Age, it is set apart to some degree by its location to the extreme southwest of England. Cornwall's predominantly rural landscape, interrupted by bleak moors, is dotted with whitewashed houses, built of stone because of a shortage of trees. Picturesque fishing villages nestle along its rocky coastline, broken by wide estuaries and craggy caves that were once a favorite for smugglers and pirates.

It is here, on the summit of a granite outcropping on an islet just off the Cornish coast, before land gives way to the Atlantic Ocean stretching out to the north, that the priory of St. Michael's Mount was built. Named for

St. Michael the Archangel, who, according to an old Cornish legend, appeared on its site to a fisherman in the fifth century, it has grown in all manner of form since its twelfth-century construction by a Benedictine abbot from Mont-St.-Michel, in Normandy, yet the massive structure maintains a cohesiveness because each addition employed the same golden-stoned granite. The Mount was later utilized as a fortress, and, in 1659, the medieval castle became the home of the St. Aubyn family.

Gothick influences were late in arriving to Cornish manor houses, such as the lovely Prideaux Place on the northern coast, where the front hall, stairs, and library, created in 1810, are typical of Strawberry Hill Gothick. This was due to a strong sense of regionalism that resulted in trends being absorbed more slowly. St. Michael's Mount, however, was the rare exception. Several particularly early Georgian Gothick rooms were constructed by the third baronet, Sir John St. Aubyn, who had been exposed to current trends as a member of Parliament serving under Robert Walpole. Sometime between 1740 and 1744, when he died, he elected to transform the disused and decaying Lady Chapel, originally built in 1463, into the elegant blue Gothick drawing room and boudoir. The lighthearted rooms are decorated with a delightful assortment of imaginative plasterwork ornamenting their walls and ceilings.

In 1954, John St. Aubyn, the present Lord St.

Levan, because of the financial burden of maintaining and preserving his unique English treasure, decided to donate the Mount, together with a generous endowment fund, to the National Trust, retaining a lease on part of the castle for his family. Now it is open throughout the year for all to savor its colorful past; a steady stream of tourists tread the narrow half-mile-long causeway connected at low tide to the village of Marazion on the Cornish coast. It is the same path followed by pilgrims who journeyed on foot—or by small open boat when the eighteen-foot tide closed off the cobbled walkway—to the early monastery, motivated in part by the promise of indulgences. More than 170,000 each year climb the steep rocky path to the imposing entrance of the splendid medieval castle.

A detail of one of the Gothick windows in the blue drawing room highlights the outstanding craftsmanship of the lovely plasterwork. The oak branch is a typical early Gothic motif.

The window valance, with its gilt wood trim, repeats the outline of the beautiful curved window panes. The shape is repeated in the arched plasterwork bordering the walls.

Left: An anteroom with vaulted ceilings has four unusual Gothick Chippendale chairs, one of which is seen here. It bears the coat of arms of the St. Aubyn and Wingfield families.

Opposite: A small bay in the boudoir, one of the Gothick rooms of St. Michael's Mount, is the perfect spot for breakfast or the time-honored English custom of afternoon tea.

Strawberry Hill

Right: Strawberry Hill's three-story façade was the first area to be renovated. This charming ogee-shaped Gothick window in the garden entry hall, one of a number of additions, has stained-glass inserts at the top taken from earlier buildings.

Opposite: The section to the left, originally the stables, and the top story of the round tower were added by Lady Waldegrave around 1860. The wrought-iron stairway leads to an anteroom dividing the nineteenth-century addition from Walpole's eighteenth-century creation on the right.

AFFLUENT RESIDENTS of London, in an effort to escape the city's heat and stench during the summer months, looked for country retreats; Twickenham, only ten miles from London on the banks of the Thames, was a favorite spot. It was here that Horace Walpole, at the age of thirty, subleased a five-acre farm bordering the Thames in 1747 from Mrs. Chenevix, the owner of a fashionable toy shop. Walpole wrote to a friend, "It is a little play-thing-house that I got out of Mrs. Chenevix's shop."[5] A year later, he purchased the property from three minors named Mortimer and promptly set about gothicizing the unpretentious house, which he had christened Strawberry Hill from old leases that referred to the ground as "Strawberry-Hill-Shot."

Strawberry Hill, Horace Walpole's villa a short distance from London, played a major role in encouraging the use of the Gothick style in residences. The ivy-covered portion of this rambling structure, ornamented with battlements, was the earliest section.

A stone screen to the side of the courtyard encloses the so-called Prior's Garden. The second-floor window to the right, which looks out to a semicircular drive and the road beyond, is in the Holbein chamber, originally used as a bedroom.

Walpole's intention was to create "a small capricious house . . . built to please my own taste, and in some degree to realize my own visions"[6]—a vision, he added, with every modern convenience. William Beckford, who built the massive Gothick Fonthill Abbey toward the end of the century, dismissed Strawberry Hill as a "gothic mousetrap."[7]

With few examples of Gothick manor houses available at mid-century, Walpole was quite free to express himself in whatever manner he chose, as he merrily altered and added as his budget allowed. As writer Linda Hewitt says, "The pursuit of Gothic afforded the thrill of discovery and the delight of improbable conjectures. Walpole used his Gothic as an intellectual plaything, a means of rising above and refuting the ordinary and mundane."[8]

His inventive, picturesque villa, with its additions and decorative motifs borrowed from a wide variety of original Gothic structures, evolved into a unique asymmetrical form that would influence the design of future English and American villas. Fancy-

ing himself an antiquarian, Walpole lifted designs from all sorts of medieval sites, from chapel tombs to cathedral choirs, applying them in a random manner to chimneypieces, ceilings, windows, balustrades, and other structures throughout his house. While Walpole's adaptations of authentic designs was a step away from Langley's whimsical inventions, their use was still purely decorative; this is especially apparent when they are compared with later nineteenth-century structural applications of Gothic forms. Victorian writer Charles Eastlake says of Strawberry Hill: "The interior . . . is just what one might expect from a man who possessed a vague admiration for Gothic without the knowledge necessary for a proper adaptation of its features. Ceilings, niches, &c., are all copied, or rather parodied, from existing examples, but with utter disregard for the original purpose of the design."[9]

Walpole assembled a "committee of taste" to assist with Strawberry Hill's makeover. John Chute, whom Walpole had met on the Grand Tour, and who, like himself, took a scholarly approach to the use of Gothic, was joined by Richard Bentley, a draftsman who provided many fanciful touches to the structure, and the gifted Swiss-born artist and scholar J. H. Muntz. Walpole also called upon a number of his other sophisticated friends, such as Robert Adam, who designed the chimneypiece and ceiling for the Round Room, which Walpole used as a drawing room.

The first renovation Walpole undertook was to the exterior, when he added a three-story bay to the east front with ogee and quatrefoil windows and a crenellated roofline trimmed with crocketed pinnacles. A new stairwell and library followed. Then, in 1758, his little villa was extended with an adjoining long gallery that ended in a round tower. The fifty-foot-long, thirteen-foot-wide picture gallery had an open cloister under it. By 1763, with the addition of a small chapel-like room referred to as the Cabinet (and later called the Tribune) just off the long gallery to display Walpole's rarer treasures, the rambling house was considered complete.

An avid art collector and a genealogist, Walpole furnished his home with assorted medieval fragments and memorabilia, from stained glass to suits of armor, to heighten the medieval ambience. Passersby intrigued with the house frequently requested a tour through it, a common practice at the time. Anxious to show off his extensive collection, Walpole opened part of Strawberry Hill to the public from noon to 3:00 P.M. May through October. Visitors flocked to tour his curious house and he took to printing tickets for admission. Walpole had used synthetic substances such as plaster in place of stone and papier-mâché as a substitute for plaster—appearance was all that mattered for early Gothicists. Strawberry Hill's gateway, based on a medieval tomb at Ely Cathedral, was constructed of artificial stone and became an annoyance, as tourists took away bits for souvenirs.

Walpole died in 1797, leaving his much-loved villa in the hands of Anne Damer, a cousin and close friend, with a yearly pension for its operation. In 1815 she relinquished it to the descendants of his niece, Countess Waldegrave, who sold Walpole's treasures at auction in 1842; it was the largest sale of the century, lasting thirty-two days. For a while it looked as though the neglected house had come to an end, but Strawberry Hill was to be a center of

Medieval armor originally lined the walls and filled niches of the stairway (opposite). The delicately carved wood balustrade was copied from a stone original leading to the Rouen Cathedral library. The left-hand door on the landing, with its canopied ceiling under triple arches, leads to the library. Poised on each of the newel posts (above) are gilded antelopes, each displaying a heraldic shield.

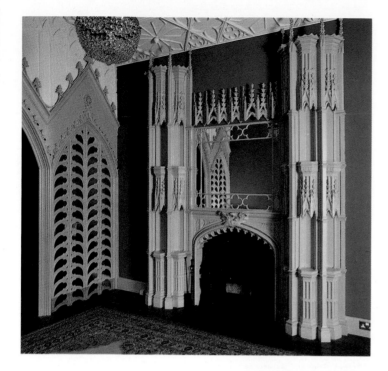

gaiety once again when the fashionable hostess Lady Waldegrave, who had married both of the countess's sons, reopened the house in 1856, supervising its restoration and the construction of a new Tudor Gothic Victorian wing in 1861. She changed the entrance but kept the original portion virtually the same, attempting to buy back paintings, furniture, and other original items from those who had purchased them at auction.

In the 1920s the property was sold to St. Mary's College and is operated by the Vincentian Order as a teachers' college. Extensive restoration under the guidance of experts from the Victoria and Albert Museum began in the late 1980s.

The Holbein chamber (above) was so called because originally it was lined with tracings from drawings of the royal Holbein portraits in Queen Caroline's closet at Kensington. The chimneypiece was inspired by the high altar at Rouen Cathedral and Archbishop Warham's tomb. A Saracen's head tops the decorative screen (right) in the Holbein chamber, while crockets and trefoils trim its pointed arches. The ribbed ceiling was copied from the Queen's dressing room at Windsor Castle.

Right: The brightly painted fireplace on one side of the small entry is ornamented with the head of a Saracen. The image is repeated throughout the house and is shown here with a heraldic shield of the Walpole family.

Below: The garden entrance opens into this small room. Painted glass collected from earlier structures was added to the tops of the door and windows to lend a touch of antiquity. The wallpaper is, appropriately, strawberry-patterned.

Above left: The elaborate chimneypiece in the library at Strawberry Hill, designed by Richard Bentley, was copied from the tomb of John of Eltham, Earl of Cornwall, in Westminster Abbey.

Above right: The painted library ceiling was designed by Walpole in the manner of ancient seals. Knights suited in armor on horseback flank a center medallion made up of a large shield encircled with smaller ones representing the families to which the Walpoles were linked by marriage.

Right: Walpole took particular pride in his library. Originally a soft gray, its painted bookcases lining the walls were inspired by a choir screen door in Old St. Paul's. Colored glass decorates

Left: Five canopied recesses finished with a gold network over mirrors run along one of the crimson-colored damask walls of Strawberry Hill's long picture gallery. The ceiling design was taken from a side aisle in Henry VII's chapel in Westminster Abbey.

Below left: The canopies, inspired by Archbishop Bouchier's tomb at Canterbury, top the niches and doors at either end of the long gallery and are festooned with trefoils based on designs by J. H. Muntz.

Below: One of the three doorways in the picture gallery, this one, based on a door in St. Alban's Abbey, leads to the small domed cabinet room, where Walpole kept his rarer treasures. He commented that it had the air of a Catholic chapel; ironically, it is now indeed a consecrated Catholic chapel.

Arbury Hall

Above: The north façade became the front entrance to Arbury Hall in 1783. A simple double-arched porte cochère, trimmed with crocketed flanking pinnacles, extends from it. The large Gothick window above lights the interior staircase.

Opposite: A riot of lace-like plaster-work embellishes the semicircular bay window ceiling, modeled on Henry VII's chapel at Westminster Abbey. Family crests ornament quatrefoils. The top portion of each window has a delicate flower motif tinted pale pink.

SOME OF THE MOST beautiful Gothick houses can be found on estates bordering the English Midlands, a region rich in coal that brought industry and great wealth to the area. Arbury Hall, just outside Nuneaton and some twenty miles south of the industrial city of Birmingham, is one of the most outstanding of the early Gothick houses as well as one of the best preserved. Many share writer Terence Davis's opinion that within Arbury's walls are "the most consummate Rococo Gothick rooms ever designed."[10]

Like a number of important English country homes, the original house was built on the foundation of an ancient priory. Its very name, Arbury Hall, is derived from the name of that Augustinian priory, which was called

Erdbury. In 1580, Sir Edmund Anderson bought the land and built a quadrangular, gabled Elizabethan house, which he exchanged six years later for Harefield Hall, then owned by John Newdegate. Newdegate then moved into Anderson's quadrangular house.

In 1750, Sir Roger Newdigate (the spelling of the family name having been changed), the fifth Baronet, who succeeded to the estate when he was fourteen, elected to update Arbury Hall in the dec-

orative Gothick style, perhaps because of his friendship with Gothick enthusiast Sanderson Miller. Newdigate, a member of Parliament for Oxford, was involved in both political and commercial endeavors. He developed coal fields on his vast estate and engineered a system of canals running through his property to link up with the national system.

A man of uncompromising patience and unswerving vision, Newdigate took fifty years to transform his family mansion. Like Walpole, Sir

Roger gathered together a collection of talented artists throughout the restoration, turning as time went on to more historic medieval structures for inspiration. Sketches done by Sir Roger indicate that he almost certainly had a hand in the design of these later sections.

Miller undoubtedly assisted in the initial designs, aided by William Hiorne, who was hired as master mason. Henry Keene, placed in charge of decorations in 1762, brought an elegant yet lighthearted touch to Arbury Hall as it was slowly transformed into a Gothick masterpiece. Keene's position of Surveyor to Westminster Abbey was especially helpful as a reference for the design of the intricate fan-vaulted ceilings—plaster castings from the Abbey were actually used for some of the detailing.

Keene was fortunate to have the services of two talented stuccoists, Robert Moor, who also executed the plasterwork at Alscot Park, and William Hanwell, who was responsible for the saloon. Keene's first assignment was to design a new drawing room, but his crowning achievement was the two-story dining room, begun in 1770. Originally it was the entrance to the great hall of the early house, and its soaring height added a sense of drama to the elegant room. The staggeringly beautiful saloon was undertaken after Keene's death in 1776 by Henry Couchman, but it bears Keene's touch and may have been influenced by his suggestions before he died.

The home of Viscount and Viscountess Daventry, the hall and its extensive grounds are open during the summer months to the public.

Opposite: Built on the site of an ancient priory, Arbury Hall is surrounded by verdant coal-rich grounds punctuated with natural and man-made lakes, canals, and a small waterfall. Its flamboyant interiors represent Gothick at its best.

Right: A copper-trimmed iron stove sits at the far end of the saloon in a small plaster alcove ornamented with an arch of open quatrefoils. Over it is a painting by Sir Joshua Reynolds. On either side of the alcove, built-in shelves display a collection of Chinese porcelain.

Above: Flowers, stars, fleurs-de-lis, leaves, and a trotting horse are all incorporated in the network of webbing that makes up the resplendent uninhibited ceiling of Arbury Hall's grand saloon.

Left: Chippendale-style Gothick chairs, with small Gothic arches marching around the seat, and arcaded chair rails line the saloon bay window. The beautiful petit-point on the chairs and settee was the handwork of Sir Roger's mother.

Opposite: The saloon is the most elaborate of Arbury Hall's rooms. An immense bay window, completed in 1798, in the final stage of gothicizing, dominates the room. Clustered columns of scagliola run up the pale walls, terminating in fan vaulting that erupts across the soaring ceiling.

Above: The central triple windows of the garden front replaced the original entrance to Arbury's great Elizabethan hall, which was converted into a two-story dining room in 1776.

Left: The dining room, occupying the grand hall of the original medieval house, is distinguished by fan vaulting, which begins three-quarters of the way up the walls and spreads across the high ceiling. Inset between slender columns are niches topped by lacy tiered canopies holding classical statuary.

Below left: Three large mullioned windows run along an aisle about ten feet deep, created by triple arches ornamented with delicate plasterwork, on the south side of the dining room. Stained-glass medallions are inset just above them.

Below right: A row of small intricate niches runs across the arched recess housing a brass-trimmed iron stove, which in . turn is centered on one wall of Arbury Hall's immense dining room, the culmination of Newdigate's Gothick restoration.

Opposite: The delightfully
decorative plasterwork of
the drawing-room walls is
continued across the barrel
ceiling, decorated with
groining and small colored
crests. A row of large
quatrefoil motifs is repeated
around the dado of
the room.

The walls of the drawing room are covered with lively plasterwork paneling
inset with family portraits, including one of Sir Richard Newdigate, the first
Baronet, to the right of the fireplace.

The marble inlaid overmantel has a large medallion framed
by ogee arches that form a scalloped trefoil. On either side of
the drawing room chimneypiece, modeled after the tomb of
Aymer de Valence in Westminster Abbey, are finial-topped
pinnacles with niches holding Chinese porcelains.

Alscot Park

Above: A detail of Gothick wood carving in the dining room.

Opposite: Alscot Park, a manor house in the heart of the Cotswolds that started life as a modest medieval cottage, was transformed in the eighteenth century with the addition of decorative battlements, turrets, and resurfaced walls of smooth ashlar stone.

SHAKESPEARE COUNTRY is the location of another remarkable Gothick gem. The manor house of Alscot Park, situated on a flat stretch of land bordering the River Stour, is a delightful example of the blending of classical and Gothick forms.

The original dwelling, which may have been owned by Deerhouse Priory in Tewkesbury, was medieval, dating back to the twelfth century. Various owners made numerous changes to the small house as it passed through the centuries, until 1749, when it was purchased as a summer retreat by James West, who held the important position of Joint Secretary to the Treasury. West's wife, the daughter of the celebrated architect Christopher Wren, after first seeing the structure, wrote to her brother,

"It was the comicallest little house you ever saw."[11] West started remodeling the simple manor house the following year, refacing its exterior walls, adding Gothick ogee arches to windows, building battlements, and, in the back of the house overlooking the river, adding a three-story bay extension.

Twelve years later, West retired and once again began remodeling his country house. This time, a major addition was made to the front of Alscot Park. It included a large entrance hall, decorated with delicate garlands, swags, and medieval arcading, and, leading off either side, a dramatic drawing room and dining room, both with intricate plasterwork on ceilings and walls. All three rooms were considerably grander than the modest existing house. Robert Moor, the stuccoist who was responsible for some of the more delicious concoctions at Arbury Hall, worked on Alscot's entrance hall and back stairway.

Interestingly, although West was an antiquarian and even served as president of the Society of Antiquaries for a time, his use of Gothick motifs had little relationship to historic references as at Strawberry Hill and Arbury Hall, leaning more heavily

Opposite: *This side view of Alscot Park, facing the dining room bay, clearly shows the Gothick addition constructed in 1762 on the left, with the lower earlier structure just behind it to the right. The River Stour winds its way past the house, creating a picturesque setting.*

Decorative eighteenth-century turrets flank Alscot Park's central porte cochère, with its heavy oak door trimmed with wood studs. The entrance was most probably added in the early nineteenth century.

toward Batty Langley's fanciful rococo Gothick style, found in the early years of the revival.

In the mid-nineteenth century, the house's glazed windows were unfortunately replaced with plate glass, which had recently been perfected and was considered at the time to be the height of fashion. James Roberts West, the descendant of the original owner who was responsible for the change, also redecorated the large dining room, removing most of the eighteenth-century plasterwork on the walls, which was far from Victorian tastes. Darkly stained oak paneling went up in its place.

In 1960 the current owners, descendants of James West, took over the three-hundred-acre family estate and began the arduous task of restoring and updating it. Furniture and carpeting found in sheds and in the attic were repaired, the drawing-room ceiling was regilded, and the dark paneling in the dining room was lightened. Structural changes also had to be made to reinforce ceilings and floors. The satisfying result of the family's labors is a comfortable environment that still retains a respect for the integrity of its ancestral home.

Above the fireplaces centered on the side walls, busts of Shakespeare and Matthew Prior rest on brackets framed by exquisite arches against a garland of oak leaves. A third bust, of Newton, is on the back wall above a doorway.

Clustered columns run up the walls of the large entrance hall. They are met by delicate pinnacled ogee arches with quatrefoils tucked below their apexes, repeating the window shapes. A large Gothick lantern extends from the center of the ceiling.

The lyrical design of the hall ceiling (below left), the work of the superb craftsman Robert Moor, is gloriously fanciful without being overly opulent. A detail of the lovely plasterwork above the fireplace reflects the eighteenth-century interest in nature (below right). Above it, a cornice of Gothick arches is joined by a romantic frieze of garlands and vases.

The staircase located behind the entrance hall is the product of early gothicizing. Its wrought-iron balustrade, the doorways, and the delicate plasterwork on walls and ceiling are a pastiche of Gothick forms.

On a landing off the stairs, a recently remodeled small room used as a study sports stenciled Gothic arches reflecting the motifs that pervade the fanciful house.

The dining room's oak paneling was the product of the
Victorian Age, when a more
serious form of Gothic
reigned. The room, now the
center of activity for the present
family, includes a small
kitchen, a sitting area around
a large fireplace, and a dining
table in the window bay.

A Tudor linenfold motif is carved into the
dining room's oak paneling. Added in the
nineteenth century and originally stained a dark
brown, it has been lightened in recent years by the
present owners.

The elegant drawing room, part of the 1764 addition, is formal, with its classical fireplace of colored marbles and Derbyshire Bluejohn frieze. Gothick elements in the room are concentrated in the pointed door frames, windows, and elaborate ceiling.

The Gothick ogee-arched doorway in Alscot Park's drawing room, with its gilded frame topped by a finial, leads out to the central entrance hallway.

A section of the ornate drawing-room ceiling, executed in papier-mâché, is composed of overlapping circles, each having a medallion within. In the center of the ceiling, the base of a pendant spreads out, recalling petals of a blossom in full bloom.

St. John the Evangelist, built in 1756, is a rare example of the use of Georgian Gothick in a church. The delightful structure at Shobdon in Herefordshire was commissioned by Viscount Bateman.

St. John the Evangelist

INTERESTINGLY, examples of ecclesiastical Georgian Gothick are quite rare. One of the most beautiful is the private church of St. John the Evangelist at Shobdon in Herefordshire, restored in the mid-1980s. It was one of several built on the site, the first dating back to the twelfth century.

Viscount Bateman of Shobdon Court was responsible for the delightful Gothick church now on the spot. His brother Richard, who was a friend of Horace Walpole, had been put in charge of the estate and supervised the church's construction, which ran from 1752 to 1756.

While St. John's architect is unknown, Michael McCarthy, in his informative recent publication, *Origins of the Gothic Revival,* speculates that it may have been the work of William Kent. Kent died in 1748, before the church was built, but its plans were initially drawn in 1746. McCarthy includes in his book an engraving done by Kent entitled "A Pulpit in the Cathedral of York," which is indeed quite similar to the one at Shobdon and

St. John's rear balcony is ornamented with a row of large quatrefoils repeating those decorating the sides of the pews. A border of pointed arches signals the start of the simple cove ceiling.

Left: Fluid lines of finial-topped ogee arches delineate windows, framing the chancel and side transepts. Clustered columns flank the altar and transept openings.

Below: Crockets outline the back of a Gothick chair in this Shobdon church. Its back, reminiscent of Gothic window tracery, is carved in pointed arches and quatrefoils.

is most convincing. An exuberant example of Gothick, its tester is ribbed with crockets and ornamented with finials.

Designed in the form of a Latin cross, St. John the Evangelist's inventive Gothick interior is beautifully refined. Between the windows, pointed arches, some with memorial tablets, are adorned with quatrefoils. Quatrefoils, a decorative motif used throughout the church, march across a rear balcony above the entrance and are repeated as decorative cutouts on the sides of pews. A simple deep cove ceiling delineated by a row of pointed arches running around the interior does not distract from the lively motifs below. Soft dove gray and white cover the pews and footstools as well as the walls.

The handsome church is a prime example of Gothick, comparable to the finest of the country houses of the period.

The exuberant Gothic pulpit in this lovely church is crowned with a crocketed tester and punctuated with decorative finials. To its left is the baptistry.

A Pulpit in the Cathedral at York.

While the church's architect is unknown, its pulpit is similar to a William Kent engraving of a pulpit in the Cathedral at York included in Some Designs of Mr. Inigo Jones and Mr. William Kent, published in 1744.

Part IV

Nineteenth-Century Castles & a Gothic Transformation

Glin Castle is an Irish Georgian house on the banks of the Shannon River. Decked out with trappings of a castle, it was probably first built in the 1780s by Colonel John Fraunceis Fitz-Gerald, the Knight of Glin, on property that had been in his family since the thirteenth century. His son added the Gothick trimmings and various Gothick lodges in the 1820s.

NCE UPON A TIME . . ." How these words were magic to our childhood ears. They had the power to carry us away on the wings of our imagination to a land of enchanted castles with valiant and charming knights ready to rescue fair damsels in distress. Not surprisingly, the Grimm brothers collected and published their beloved fairy tales, familiar to generations of children, in the early nineteenth century, when Gothic was flourishing—a style closely associated with a time when knighthood was in flower and one that took special delight in the imagination.

Castles, whether from the pages of a storybook or from real life, have traditionally held a unique appeal for all ages. Rose Macaulay, in *Pleasure of Ruins,* writes, "The castle has always been a formidable image, a powerful, intimidating fantasy of the human imagination."[1] The Norman Conquest in 1066 heralded the first great era of castle building, with massive defensive structures dominating many English towns and villages during the warring Middle Ages. Architectural elements such as battlements, turrets, lancet windows, and drawbridges all evolved out of the need for protection. By the seventeenth century, however, with the countryside more secure, fortresses began to be replaced by country manor houses.

Images of castles returned to the English countryside in the early decades of the eighteenth century, under the guise of decaying miniature castles ornamenting landscape gardens. By the close of the century, castle building was once again undertaken in earnest. But while these baronial residences had a distinctly medieval flavor, their construction was motivated purely by the romantic appeal of the Middle Ages rather than by a desire to actually reproduce an original Norman stronghold.

Castle building became the ultimate expression of the Picturesque Movement of the late eighteenth century. What started as a philosophical concept associated with landscape gardens was adapted to architecture when Richard Payne Knight, a major supporter of the Picturesque Movement, consciously utilized the principles of the picturesque in his decidedly Gothick Downton Castle in East Cowes. Starting in 1774, Knight constructed a large irregularly formed structure specifically designed as an integral part of the surrounding landscape.

The lure of many of the imposing newly built castles was heightened by their romantic settings in dramatic spots that dominated the landscape. The Scottish Culzean Castle, positioned on the rugged cliffs of the Ayrshire coast overlooking the sea, was just such a location. Architect Robert Adam, better known for his classical tastes, was responsible for its design, which incorporated a considerably older mansion house. While the use of many Gothic architectural elements was not particularly popular in Scottish houses, Scotland's rough landscape was aptly suited to the dramatic, solitary aspects of castles.

The Gothick castle appealed to the wild and romantic Irish also, and, as in Scotland, it melded well with the rugged Irish landscape. Wealthy Irish landowners encountering Gothick on visits to English country houses had brought the style home with them. The grounds of many substantial Irish houses abounded with authentic medieval ruins, many of them in the southwest. Consequently, the fashion for adding decorative turrets and battlements to contemporary dwellings was quite easily

acceptable because it incorporated familiar forms. Gothic's reappearance in Ireland was at Moore Abbey in the 1760s, but according to *Burke's Guide to Country Houses*, Gothick "was not really fashionable until immediately after the Union, when Gothic castles suddenly became all the rage."[2] With the passing of the Act of Union in 1800, which abolished the Irish Parliament and joined England and Ireland in a legislative union, a great deal of castellating went on. The castle of Charlesville Forest, started in 1800, and Luttrellstown are two excellent examples.

Some eighteenth- and nineteenth-century castles were built from scratch, but many originally started life as Georgian houses. Glin Castle, on the western coast of Ireland in County Limerick, is a prime example. Soon after his marriage in 1812, John Fraunceis Fitz-Gerald, the Knight of Glin, added battlements to his eighteenth-century home, gothicizing a wing of the house and farm buildings with crenellations and adding three Gothick lodges a few years later.

In England, the rugged Cornish coast was the site of John Nash's imposing Caeyrhays Castle, built in 1808. Nash, who was responsible for the exotic Brighton Pavilion, designed a number of Gothick castles, including Koepp in Sussex, Lascombe in Devon, and his own castle at East Cowes on the Isle of Wight in 1790. James Wyatt, an enthusiast of the Gothick style and a rival of Nash's, built Norris Castle on the Isle of Wight about the same time. Wyatt was considered by many to be the most fashionable architect in England; in 1796, two years after tackling the monumental Fonthill Abbey, he was appointed Surveyor General to the Office of the Works, the most exalted post an architect could hold.

The rebuilding of Windsor Castle became the most important of Wyatt's projects. By the time the Prince of Wales, at the age of fifty-seven, assumed the title of King George IV, Windsor Castle had fallen into grave disrepair. The State Apartments, suffering the effects of an assortment of influences as each monarch put his or her stamp on them, needed not only modernizing but unifying as well. Wyatt gothicized part of the exterior of the State Apartments and the Main Hall; upon his death, his nephew Jeffry Wyattville, who changed his name after being knighted for his services at the castle, assumed the task, and from 1824 to 1830 he carried on, gothicizing the staircase, the Waterloo Chamber, the Knights of the Garter Throne Room, and the Queen's Guard Chamber.

The restoration of Windsor Castle inspired many to construct smaller versions on their country estates and to update earlier castles with currently fashionable Gothic motifs. Sir Charles Barry, prize-winning architect of the Houses of Parliament, and a number of his contemporaries, such as Anthony Salvin, Robert Smirke, and Edward Blore, were responsible for the design of many remodeled or newly built castles of the early Victorian period. In Wales, Lord Bute, one of the wealthiest men in England, aided by architect William Burges, rebuilt Cardiff Castle (see page 157) and the smaller Castell Coche. One of the great triumphs of nineteenth-century Romantic architecture, Cardiff Castle is brimming with ornate Victorian Gothic ornamentation. Castle Drago, the last great castle to be built in England, was designed by the renowned architect Sir Edwin Lutyens in the early years of the twentieth century for Sir Julius Drewe, founder of a grocery chain.

This watercolor of Park House in Cardiff, designed by architect William Burges, was done by Axel Haig about 1872. It is typical of the High Victorian Gothic popular during the second half of the nineteenth century, with ornamentation eliminated and colored banding around windows and doors for decorative interest.

While architect A.W. N. Pugin was unsuccessful in his efforts to suppress the taste for picturesque castles, he was ultimately instrumental in bringing a close to Gothick's early exuberance. Reinforced by the 1833 Oxford Movement, favoring a return to Catholic doctrines and practices within the Church of England, and bolstered by the remodeling of Windsor Castle and the rebuilding of the Houses of Parliament in the 1850s as well as an expanding social conscience, a more serious form of Gothic was to become the most important design direction of the mid-nineteenth century.

By the 1840s, with Queen Victoria now on the throne, the use of Gothic went through a transformation, turning from decorative and associational to a concern for archaeological and structural accuracy. With its romantic youth now at an end, in becoming more authentic it became decidedly less adventurous. While the linear Perpendicular Style was at first more popular, Victorians a bit later in the century preferred earlier medieval Gothic forms exemplified by heavier shapes and simpler detailing.

The Victorians, who took not only themselves but life in general very seriously, adopted this same attitude when choosing architecture. Classical designs, except when utilized for municipal buildings, were rejected because of their connection to what was viewed as the decadent Regency period. Gothic, on the other hand, appealed to the class-conscious wealthy English because of its suggestion of ancient lineage, and appealed as well to the growing middle class, who turned to a style rooted firmly in England's history for identity.

When the Houses of Parliament were destroyed by the Great Fire of 1834, the Perpendicular Style of Gothic was selected for its redesign in an effort to retain a cohesive connection with the eleventh-century Gothic Westminster Hall that survived. Sir Charles Barry was awarded the job; he was ably assisted by A. W. N. Pugin, who was responsible for the exterior and interior detailing.

Augustus Welby Northmore Pugin, born in 1812, was perhaps the most influential of the nineteenth-century personalities in advancing and redirecting the Gothic Revival. At twenty-two Pugin converted to Catholicism, and his new religion was to play an important role in his life. Pugin's father, Augustus Claudius Pugin, a French émigré who had worked for the architect John Nash, made extensive studies of medieval buildings, publishing *Specimens of Gothic Architecture* in 1821. His *Examples of Gothic Architecture,* a three-volume handbook of mathematically accurate drawings, was completed by his son

A GOTHIC WINDOW.

after his death. An invaluable tool for architects, these books proved to be a turning point in the Gothic Revival.

The younger Pugin was intense, intolerant, and dogmatic; he believed Gothic to be the only appropriate architectural style for Christians, insisting on strict archaeological correctness as well as on truthful construction and the use of ornamentation only as it related to a structure. Ultimately, architecture was to be judged according to the morality and religion of its creator.

Pugin had a successful metalworking factory and stained-glass business. His excellent memory for visual details was valuable in the design of furniture, fabric, wallpaper, and tiles, all of which he based on medieval precedent. In 1835, Pugin designed and built St. Marie's Grange outside Salisbury for his family; a new form of Gothic eliminating any super-

ficial ornamentation, it set an example for smaller mid-Victorian houses. Of the more than one hundred buildings Pugin designed, most were churches.

Pugin first put forward his principle that Christianity and Gothic were synonymous in *Contrasts; or A Parallel Between the Architecture of the 14th and 15th Centuries and Similar Buildings of the Present Day,* an 1836 pamphlet. Initially drawn to the Perpendicular Style, he turned to the simplified form of the Middle Pointed period shortly thereafter. *True Principles of Pointed or Christian Architecture,* published in 1841, deplored the earlier Gothick of Wyatt and the castles of the Picturesque Movement. Pugin came to a sad end in 1852 at the age of forty. Having driven himself to excessive limits, he died overworked and insane.

Contemporaries of Pugin, such as G. E. Street, William Butterfield, and William Burges, among the most eminent architects of the day, were also

The most influential of the early-nineteenth-century publications on furniture was Ackermann's Repository of the Arts, *which appeared monthly from January 1809 until December 1828. These Gothic furniture engravings by Augustus W. N. Pugin were included in 1825 and 1826. Shown on these two pages are (left to right) a Gothic window, hall lamp and hall chairs, sofa, and bed.*

exponents of High Victorian Gothic. In an attempt to modernize Gothic, many incorporated constructional polychroming, a style that made use of decorative colored brickwork and tiles, in their buildings. Street's 1855 book, *Brick and Marble in the Middle Ages,* served as a reference for what became known as Italian or High Victorian Gothic. But the person most responsible for popularizing the style was not an architect.

John Ruskin, an architectural historian and a naturalist, had an outstanding command of the English language coupled with a passionate conviction of the importance of architecture. Born in 1819, Ruskin adopted Pugin's preachings, which instilled architecture with moral and ethical qualities, yet the staunchly Protestant Ruskin had little liking for the Catholic Pugin. On numerous trips to Italy, Ruskin was impressed by its medieval architecture and wrote in praise of it in *The Stones of Venice* in 1853. Keenly aware of the importance of color in architecture, he created an interest in Venetian Gothic with his eloquent praise of its technique of colored banding, created by using contrasting material to form moldings.

Featured here are engravings from the popular 1808 publication A Collection of Designs for Household Furniture and Interior Decoration, *by George Smith, which included a number of plates "after the Gothic or Old English Fashion."*

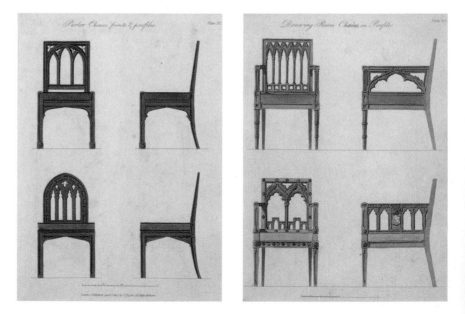

A six-inch-high 1840 English salt-glaze teapot is ornamented with designs of the Apostles, a common motif of the time.

An English brass watch stand and bottle holder, ten inches high, has the façade of a cathedral.

Gothic arches are repeated in rows across this Wilton carpet, an 1848 reproduction that duplicates the colors of one in the archival files of Woodward Grosvenor, the company that produced the carpet for Burrows & Co. The border was not part of the original overall design.

By the mid-nineteenth century, Gothic motifs found their way into virtually all areas of the decorative arts, including ceramics, glassware and silverware, lighting, and even metal stoves. Gothic and Elizabethan furniture designs, used primarily in grand halls and libraries, were at first custom-made for specific houses but later simplified versions were mass-produced for cottage dwellers. By 1830, inlays, marquetry, and exotic woods, which captured the fancy of Regency England, were usurped by rosewood, mahogany, walnut, and oak. Pugin brought out *Gothic Furniture* in 1835.

Flamboyant Gothic designs on wallpaper and fabric started appearing in the eighteenth century, with patterns employing vistas of ruins, arches, quatrefoils, and tracery, and by 1815 were quite common. Carpets as well were designed with Gothic motifs throughout the 1830s and '40s. Gothic-style draperies topped with valances and pelmets that followed the line of a Gothic arch, which were frequently embellished with embroidery of Gothic ornaments, were commonly used in dining rooms or libraries.

During the last half of the nineteenth century, there were several movements formed by artists and craftsmen, such as the Pre-Raphaelite Brotherhood, that were an outgrowth of Gothic influences; they incorporated medieval themes, an interest in nature, and the ideals of excellence of design, integrity of materials, and exacting craftmanship. "By the 1870's," as Gavin Stamp and Andre Goulancourt noted in their book *The English House 1860–1914*, "avant-garde architects had abandoned the literal Gothic style—the pointed arch which had so obsessed Pugin—. . . but they essentially remained Gothicists in their approach to design."[3]

Birr Castle

GOTHICK MADE its presence known in Ireland around 1800; one of the best examples of Irish Gothick can be found at romantic Birr Castle in County Offaly. Situated in the heart of Ireland, the town of Birr sidles up against the castle wall to the east of the 130-acre desmesne, or park, while on its western front the land rises, then drops sharply down to the lively Camcor River.

The ancestral home of the Earls of Rosse, Birr Castle started with the purchase of 1,277 acres of land in 1620 by English-born Sir Laurence Parsons, who had come to Ireland thirty years before with his brother. Parsons promptly started altering a gatehouse on the property by connecting two free-standing seventeenth-century towers to it. The structure suffered extensive damage during the turbulent second half of the seventeenth century, passing down through several generations of Parsonses to Sir Laurence, the second Earl of Rosse, who inherited his title in 1807.

Sir Laurence had been a member of the Irish House of Commons and supported an independent self-governing Ireland loyal to the crown. When the Act of Union was passed in 1800, Parsons retired to his estate at Birr, where he began extensive remodeling and updating, much of it in the then-fashionable Gothick style, which was largely inspired by work being undertaken at the castle of Charleville Forest. Sir Laurence was actively in-

Opposite: Tapestries line the walls of Birr Castle's entrance hall, built over the original entrance. Its Tudor ceiling was added around 1838, while its exquisite large Gothick window, draped in green velvet and overlooking a lush rear garden, is from an earlier remodeling.

Right: The wardrobe, mirror, chairs, stools, and jardiniere in the master bedroom were designed by Mary Rosse and made by the estate workshops for her marriage to the third Earl in 1836.

volved in the designs; one of his notebooks contains drawings for the castle's castellated front entrance, which was remodeled in 1810. The spectacular Gothick saloon overlooking the river was also undertaken at this time. A plan for a Gothick staircase has been found but it was never executed.

Sir Laurence was known and respected for his honesty and intelligence. His son William became one of the most distinguished astronomers of his day, building a reflection telescope on the grounds of Birr, which, until 1917, was the world's largest. In keeping with the castle renovations, the telescope's walls were embellished with Gothic arches and topped with crenellations. William's wife, Mary, was a pioneer in the field of photography. Charles, the youngest of their eleven children, invented the steam turbine.

Changes were again on the agenda after a fire destroyed the roof of the castle in 1832. A third story was built, and Gothick plasterwork was added to the staircase. Third-floor corridors were vaulted and a Gothick ceiling installed in the entrance hall. In the 1840s, new Gothick gates were constructed and moats and fortifications rebuilt, motivated in part by a desire to provide employment to many in the area during the famine.

Restoration to the castle and careful maintenance of the vast landscaped park, as well as cataloguing the extensive collection of documents pertaining to the estate, is an ongoing job for the present Lord Rosse, who has dedicated his energies to preserving Birr. Its magnificent gardens, among the most beautiful found anywhere, are open to the public throughout the year.

Birr's resplendent octagonal saloon is an outstanding example of the inventive Gothick spirit. Three Gothick windows embellished with delicate tracery stretch from floor to ceiling along the far wall, while slender gold-and-white columns rise up the other walls, flocked in green and gold, to a splendid vaulted tent-like ceiling.

Opposite: The saloon fireplace is detailed with Gothick motifs. Reflected in the ornate gilded mirror above it is a beautiful Waterford crystal chandelier suspended from the center of the room and one of the large Gothick windows that line the opposite wall.

A detail of the elaborately carved Gothick pelmet and velvet drapery in Birr Castle's darkly opulent dining room.

The dining room plasterwork and the pelmets trimming its great bay window date from the second quarter of the nineteenth century. In the 1940s, Anne Rosse was responsible for resurrecting the imposing ormolu chandelier, redoing the paneling, and covering the walls with flocked damask-like wallpaper.

An overscaled egg-and-dart molding frames doorways and the bay window in the regal Gothic dining room at Birr Castle.

The beautiful dining room doorknobs are embellished with the initial "R," representing the Earls of Rosse.

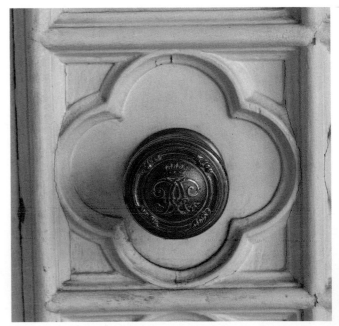

Eastnor Castle

Above: Craftsmanship was high on the list of priorities for Pugin. The beautiful detailing of the brass doorknobs, with their stylized flower and leaf ornamentation, speaks volumes.

Opposite: Magnificent tapestries line the walls of the 1849 drawing room. Designed by A. W. N. Pugin, it is a sterling example of the more serious approach Gothic veered toward by the mid-nineteenth century. The chandelier is a copy of one in Nuremberg Cathedral.

THE IMPOSING Eastnor Castle in Ledbury, Herefordshire, designed by architect Robert Smirke, was begun in March of 1812 and completed six years later. It was commissioned by the romantic John, the first Earl of Somers, and is sited on a hilltop with commanding views of the Malvern Hills. Its grounds include a three-hundred-acre park across a small lake just below the castle, with red deer and unusual examples of flora and fauna.

In keeping with the spirit of the castle, the Great Hall is lined with ancient suits of armor and weaponry. Just off it is the entrance to the splendid Gothic drawing room, the product of renowned architect A. W. N. Pugin. The grandly proportioned room is distinguished by richly gilded

fan vaulting, pendants, and decorative designs on ceiling and walls. Commissioned by the second Earl in 1849, it is a wonderful example of the more serious approach to Gothic in mid-nineteenth-century Victorian England. While still flamboyant, the ornamentation is more grounded in historic references than the earlier exuberance of the eighteenth-century Gothick of Arbury Hall and Strawberry Hill.

One of the particularly special qualities about dwellings, like Eastnor, that have been handed down through generations of the same family is that many still possess their original furnishings, providing a rare opportunity to savor unique interiors imprinted with the eccentricities of centuries of occupants. Eastnor's Gothic drawing room is filled with fine furniture, exquisite Brussels tapestries, and works

of art. Pugin was responsible for the design of a number of the furnishings, such as the Gothic bookcase, inlaid round table, velvet-covered chairs, and the spectacular brass chandelier, first shown at the Great Exhibition of 1851.

Heraldic emblems of the Somers and Cocks family are emblazoned around the drawing room. Above the large fireplace, the Somers family motto, "Be useful rather than conspicuous," is displayed along with a heraldic tree illustrating the family genealogy from the time of Thomas Cocks of Bishops Cleeve, whose son Richard, around 1600, bought the property on which part of the castle is built. In 1695, Richard's son Charles married Mary Somers, who brought with her a substantial fortune; it was their grandson, John, who built Eastnor Castle.

Above left: Virginia creeper climbs the walls of Eastnor Castle, bringing touches of flaming red in the fall. In keeping with the fashion of the day, this early-nineteenth-century castle was constructed to look as though it could have entertained the Knights of the Round Table.

Above right: The lofty curved ceiling of the drawing room is ornamented with rich painting and pendants. A Tudor linenfold motif is repeated in the dado around the room. Above the heavily carved fireplace is the family coat of arms, with interlocking family trees.

Right: Simple columns join elaborate gilded and richly painted vaulting that fans out across the drawing room ceiling, while various gilded leaf-like moldings edge the doors and ceiling. The letter "S" scattered throughout stands for the Somers family, whose coat of arms and motto are painted above the door.

Cardiff Castle

Right: The Winter Smoking Room door in Cardiff Castle is decorated with marquetry. In an upper panel, at the top of a tree, sits a Stuart lion bearing the arms of Stuart of Bute. Birds, some on branches, sing to the music of a drum and harp played by a squirrel and mouse. The door handle is in the form of a bird.

Opposite: The walls of the octagonal staircase in the old watch tower, with its circular stairs, present a fantastical version of the Middle Ages, with roundels scattered among a leaflike motif, illustrating scenes from Aesop's fables. A muzzled lion sits on the newel post.

THE ULTIMATE expression of Victorian Gothic lies within the walls of Cardiff Castle. Its interiors are, in the opinion of respected historian Mark Girouard, "among the most remarkable and impressive achievements of the 19th-century Gothic Revival."[4] Distinguished by a sense of fantasy based on a highly romanticized vision of the Middle Ages, the castle interiors are, nevertheless, worlds away from Arbury Hall and the other confections created one hundred years earlier.

Cardiff Castle, an amalgam of styles from medieval times through the end of the nineteenth century, is situated near the River Taff in the heart of the Welsh capital, Cardiff. The earliest building on the site was a Roman fort dating from around 75 A.D. A Norman defense curtain was later erected on top, with living quarters added in the fifteenth century. The low, massive walls of the castle's austere and military-like exterior belie the elaborate splendor of its interiors. Writer Olive Cook comments, "Not only must they be among the most lavish ever created, but they shock the senses with the boldness, the unrelenting thoroughness, the sustained, almost maniacal energy with which every detail of the unique decoration has been carried out."[5]

The immense structure passed through the hands of a number of powerful British families until, in 1776, much in need of repair, it came into the possession of John Stuart, first Marquess of Bute, who hired Henry Holland to reconstruct the decaying lodgings in the Georgian Gothick style. But it was his great-grandson, John Patrick Crichton-Stuart, third Marquess of Bute, who was to bring about major changes, embarking upon a building program that lasted for sixty years. His father, who had died when he was six months old, left him one of the largest estates in Great Britain. Recognizing the need for a port to handle the expanding iron and coal industry in South Wales, he had sunk his fortune into developing Bute Docks. They would turn Cardiff into an important commercial world port and a major city. Sophia, second Marchioness, was to die in 1859, when her son was twelve.

One of the first decisions of the serious, shy, and scholarly third Marquess upon coming into his inheritance in 1868 was to undertake the reconstruction of Cardiff Castle, a small portion of his vast property. He had enlisted the talented, quirky architect William Burges, considered by many to be the greatest exponent of High Victorian Gothic, to propose a scheme to restore the castle's living quarters in 1865. A scholar like his patron, Burges was fascinated with the Middle Ages, going so far as to

have a set of clothes appropriate to the period made up, which he wore on occasion. Burges's preference was for French thirteenth-century Gothic rather than the English Decorated period favored by Pugin.

Construction began with the turreted clock tower at the southwestern corner, consisting of summer and winter smoking rooms together with the bachelor bedroom, which form the bachelor suite. Three other towers were enlarged and heightened. Bright murals depicting scenes from the life of one of the Norman lords of the castle top the wainscoted walls of Burges's elaborate banqueting hall. Arches with elaborate crocketing form over doorways, while stained-glass windows depict many of the castle's past owners. Fan vaults create a banding around the decorated timber ceiling, with rows of carved angels just above it.

The third Marquess did not stop at Cardiff Castle but went on to build and restore numerous structures throughout Britain, lending credence to his reputation as one of Britain's greatest builders. Cardiff Castle was donated to the city in 1947 and is open to the public throughout the year.

The third Marquess turned a study, a favorite retreat of his father, the second Marquess, into a private chapel and dedicated it to him. The large central windows depict four apostles.

OMNIA VINCIT AMOR ET NOS CEDAMVS AMOR

The theme of the Winter Smoking Room is time. Stained-glass windows celebrate the days of the week. Zodiacal figures adorn walls and vaulted ceiling. Above the chimney-piece, autumn pursuits of harvesting and hawking are illustrated. The red leather door leading into the Winter Smoking Room (right) is covered with an overlay of ornate gilded ironwork decorated with birds. A border framing the door picks up the bird motif.

Arrows descending from stylized clouds rain down the Winter Smoking Room's gilded chimneypiece hood (opposite). The carved figure of Love, supported by Capricorn, the zodiacal figure of the winter months, is joined by a frieze depicting winter amusements for lovers. The Latin inscription translates, "Love conquers all, let us yield to love."

Above: The staircase walls are painted in a stylized motif simulating tile and limestone and include illustrations of animals and birds, reflecting Lord Bute's love of natural history. Overhead, a riot of bold color and motifs ornament the lively vaulted ceiling.

Opposite: The banqueting hall, just off the top of the circular stairs, is rich in symbolism. Based on the life of Robert, Earl of Gloucester, the chimneypiece replicates a castle gatehouse and forms the focal point of the room. Scattered about the chimneypiece are small figures such as a lady bidding farewel to a knight on horseback.

Part V

The Arrival of Gothic in the United States

URING THE EARLY YEARS of the nineteenth century, as America was adjusting to its newly won freedom, Gothic influences struggled for a foothold. But it was far from love at first sight for a nation grounded in the Puritan ethic. Simple unadorned Colonial and conservative Federal houses whose designs were based on rules that governed proportion and order were very much in favor.

It was during the 1830s that a revolution in architecture began transforming the American landscape. The acceptance of the picturesque Gothic, while not as all-consuming as in England, brought a vitality to American architecture. Breaking free from the conforming restraints of symmetrical forms dictated by earlier styles, the Gothic style encouraged experimentation. What emerged was a style distinctly American, one that gave free reign to the imagination. As William Pierson, Jr., states in *American Buildings and Their Architects,* "The Gothic house changed the face of the American town, and shattered forever the simplicity and stylistic coherence of a deeply rooted classical tradition."[1]

The Gothic style was used in a rich diversity of structures, from rustic cottages to castle-like villas strongly influenced by the combined efforts of architect Alexander Jackson Davis and landscape designer and writer Andrew Jackson Downing. By the time Gothic was established in the United States, its early, more whimsical days were left behind and it had headed into its Picturesque phase. Whereas a number of architects had flirted with Gothic toward the end of the eighteenth century, adding touches of it to decidedly classical structures, its use in residences was still rare. An early example was Sedgeley, built in 1799 on a bank of the Schuylkill River outside Philadelphia and demolished in 1857. Designed by English-born architect Benjamin Henry Latrobe, the symmetrical house was decked out in pointed arches and hood moldings combined with neoclassical motifs. Latrobe, who came to America after the death of his wife, was the most prominent of a number of architects who emigrated during the Federal period.

Unlike English Gothick, which reappeared in the eighteenth century in domestic architecture (adopted by gentlemen of comfortable means who were drawn to its aesthetic qualities), American Gothic got its start in ecclesiastical buildings. By the 1820s Gothic was frequently selected for churches of all denominations and even an occasional synagogue and Masonic temple. Many of the churches were unpretentious wooden buildings with pointed windows and doors, a square tower, and a steep gable roof. The New York Ecclesiastical Society, founded in 1847 by the growing Episcopal Church in America, controlled the design of many rural churches, selecting Gothic partly because it was less expensive to construct.

English-born Richard Upjohn, the leading Gothic Revival church architect, was responsible for some of this country's finest churches. He designed a number of smaller churches inspired by those found in English villages. In an effort to encourage design excellence in rural areas, he published designs for churches, schoolhouses, and parsonages in *Upjohn's Rural Architecture* in 1852. Trinity Church in New York City was Upjohn's most important work. Completed in 1846, it is one of three Gothic churches looked upon today as among the most important architectural achievements of the nineteenth century. Ithiel Town's Trinity Church in

Sedgeley, the 1799 Philadelphia residence of William Crammond, is shown in this engraving by William Birch from County Seats of the U.S. and North America. *Designed by Benjamin Latrobe, it was the first American house to incorporate Gothic architecture elements.*

WEST END   EAST END

Richard Upjohn's charming simple nave church with bellcote, designed in 1848 for St. Paul's Church in Brookline, Massachusetts, was never built because parishioners wanted something more elaborate. A number of similar Upjohn churches were constructed and proved to be influential in the design of churches at the time.

New Haven, finished in 1817, and James Renwick, Jr.'s St. Patrick's Cathedral in New York City, built in the English Decorated style, are the other two. St. Patrick's, the largest church in America at the time, comparable in scale as well as grandeur to the magnificent cathedrals throughout Europe, was completed in 1879, with the exception of its spires, which took another nine years to finish.

By the 1830s, inviting examples of domestic Gothic started appearing across the American landscape. While it had arrived by way of England, once on American soil Gothic was to dance to its own tune. This distinct difference was the result of a number of factors. Unlike America, which had boundless wilderness, English landscape gardens could only attempt to create the illusion of untamed landscape. Choices of building materials varied as well—eighteenth-century English residences were frequently of stone because wood was scarce, while in the United States there was a bounty of natural resources such as timber.

English pattern books from such authors as Batty Langley, Thomas Chippendale, and John Claudius Loudon were important sources for American architects, furniture makers, and local carpenters, playing a part in the acceptance of Gothic in America. But it was the romantic novels of Sir Walter Scott, first published in the United States in the 1830s, and widely distributed and devoured by Americans hungry for diversion, that ultimately sparked the imagination of the nation, creating a wave of enthusiasm for Gothic. Scott's descriptive tales of chivalry and valor set in the Middle Ages were taken to heart by a country engulfed in a romantic spirit. Scott's writings inspired the work of a number of American writers and poets, such as Edgar Allan Poe, James Fenimore Cooper, William Cullen Bryant, and Washington Irving, many of

whom made the pilgrimage to Abbotsford, Scott's romantic baronial castle on the River Tweed in Scotland. Irving's charming Dutch manor house, Sunnyside, and Cooper's classic Otsego Hall, remodeled by inventor Samuel Morse, incorporated a number of Gothic elements.

Robert Gilmor is credited with building the first truly Gothic house in America. Born into a wealthy Maryland family, Gilmor traveled to France as an attaché to the American embassy after graduating from Harvard. While in Europe, with the prerequisite papers of introduction in hand, he paid a visit to Sir Walter Scott at his celebrated home. Upon returning to America, Gilmor commissioned the leading architectural firm of Town and Davis in 1832 to build a replica of Abbotsford, naming it Glenellen after his wife, Ellen Ward. (Glenellen was one of two Gothic-inspired houses designed by Town and Davis in 1832. Davis recorded another 1832 commission for a Gothic house for James Moulton of Brooklyn, New York, which he referred

to as the first Gothic villa in the United States, but no drawings or other evidence of it has survived.)

Irregular in form, Glenellen's castellated towers and walls were of stone quarried on the estate. It even had a sham ruin gatehouse. Gilmor ran short of funds, however, and plans for the top floor had to be scrapped. In 1988, Glenellen burned to the ground, having been abandoned and neglected for some time.

Alexander Jackson Davis started his career as an architectural illustrator, joining Ithiel Town as a junior partner in 1829. The combination of the older, established Town, an engineer possessing one of the most important architectural libraries in the country, and the ambitious, younger Davis proved to be a successful partnership, which lasted until 1835 and was briefly resurrected in 1842. Davis, who grew up with a love of books, now had a treasure trove of material at his fingertips, which undoubtedly helped to broaden his knowledge of Gothic.

Town's architectural preference was for Greek

Glenellen, set in the Maryland countryside twelve miles outside of Baltimore, was the romantic home of Robert Gilmor. This asymmetrical house, built in 1832 and credited with being the first truly Gothic house in the U.S., was the work of the architectural team of Town & Davis.

Opposite: English pattern books were turning out beautifully illustrated engravings of Gothic country villas—such as this one from Francis Goodwin's 1833 publication, Domestic Architecture—that were an influence on American architects.

Small hall chairs accompany a lovely dressing glass and a two-drawer dressing table ornamented with large quatre-foils; all, c. 1840–50, are in mahogany. On the wall, a trompe l'œil wallpaper border from Brunschwig & Fils imitates stonework. Furniture included in the Houston Museum's 1976 Gothic Revival show.

This colored engraving features a perspective of the Nathan B. Warren Troy cottage and its surrounding grounds. Constructed in 1838, it is one of the many dwellings designed by A. J. Davis to meet the needs of middle-class Americans interested in a home of their own.

A drawing shows the east elevation of Wildmont Lodge, A. J. Davis's romantic twenty-acre summer residence at Eagle Rock in Orange, New Jersey, built in 1878. The cliff-top retreat had a spectacular view, which extended as far as New York City.

Revival; he and Davis played a major role in its use for public buildings, but, as Davis was to write in his book *Rural Residences,* "The Greek Temple form, perfect in itself and well adapted as it is to public edifices, and even to town mansions, is inappropriate for country residences."[2] Drawn instead to the picturesque quality as well as the versatility of Gothic, the prolific Davis was soon to become Gothic's major advocate as well as one of the most popular architects of the day. His imaginative designs encapsulated the spirit of the age, inspiring countless cottages throughout the land.

Davis published two thin installments of *Rural Residences Etc. Consisting of Designs, Original and Selected, for Cottages, Farm-Houses, Villas, and Village Churches* in 1837. Its introduction read, "The following series of designs has been prepared in compliance with the wishes of a few gentlemen who are desirous of seeing a better taste prevail in the Rural Architecture of this country." It continued, "The bold, uninteresting aspect of our houses must be obvious to every traveller; and to those who are familiar with the picturesque cottages and villas of England."[3] The book, the first of its kind in America, introduced the concept of the villa to American architecture.

While *Rural Residences* had a limited distribution, it was most favorably received. It featured hand-colored lithographs of three architectural styles termed classical, hybrid, and Gothic. Davis's preference was for the last, which he called English collegiate style, because "it admits of greater variety both of plan and outline; —is susceptible of additions from time to time, while its bay windows, oriels, turrets, and chimney shafts give a pictorial effect to the elevation."[4] *Rural Residences* included a drawing of a whimsical gate lodge at Blithewood, a large stone house built in the Gothic style in the mid-1830s; this gatehouse was to become the proto-type of the American Gothic cottage (see page 175).

Davis was responsible for the Gothic design of the Wadsworth Atheneum in Hartford, Connecticut, and the Virginia Military Institute. He designed several residences in Manhattan, such as W. H. Coventry Waddell's picturesque villa with turrets, battlements, and oriel windows, built in 1844 at Thirty-seventh Street and Fifth Avenue and demolished only thirteen years later to make way for the Brick Presbyterian Church. Davis rescued its staircase, incorporating it into Wildmont, a summer house he had built for his family in 1856. His Gothic House of Mansions, a series of eleven connecting houses built in 1858, which later became Rutgers Female College, was just a few blocks north at Fifth Avenue and Forty-second Street.

In 1838, Alexander Jackson Davis met Andrew Jackson Downing. Four years earlier, at nineteen, Downing had joined his brother in a Newburgh, New York, nursery, a business their father had owned and operated before his death. Andrew became its sole proprietor five years later. Within a relatively short time he was looked upon as one of America's leading landscape gardeners and horticulturists. Downing's 1845 publication, *The Fruits and Fruit Trees of America,* considered the definitive work on the subject in the United States, played a role in standardizing the names of fruits. He was to become a major architectural critic and theorist as well before his tragic death at age thirty-six.

Motivated by a concern over a general lack of harmony between American houses and their settings, Downing used his considerable talent as a writer to persuade a receptive American public that a house and its setting should be viewed as a cohesive unit. Passionately persistent, he encouraged the construction of houses that were positioned to take full advantage of a picturesquely enhanced landscape.

The handsome Downing, who had married into one of Newburgh's most important families, dedicated his first book, published in 1841, to his wife's great uncle, ex-President John Quincy Adams. The first book of its kind written in the United States, *A Treatise on the Theory and Practise of Landscape Gardening, Adapted to North America; with a View to the Improvement of Country Residences* went through repeated reprintings, bringing Downing a major step closer to convincing the country that landscaping was within the reach of every homeowner.

While Downing's book discussed several architectural styles, his favorite was Tudor Gothic and a simplified version of it that he referred to as Rural Gothic, or the English cottage style, because it "gives character and picturesque expression to many landscapes entirely devoid of that quality." Highland Gardens, Downing's own Tudor Gothic house in Newburgh, New York, overlooking the Hudson and, sadly, torn down in 1951, was illustrated in *A Treatise*.

Downing was twenty-three when he met Davis, twelve years older and by then a highly successful architect. Sharing a mutual commitment to developing an architecture that would be suitable to the American life-style, they proved to be a perfect match. Both were romantics to the core; drawn to the emotional aspects of the Picturesque, they believed it to be an appropriate expression of the young country's tastes and ideals. Their vision was to change the course of American domestic architecture.

Downing collaborated with Davis on three popular architectural books. Each covered the practical aspects of the field as well as the aesthetic, offering explicit information and specific advice. Written in an easily readable style, they also featured plans and elevations of houses. Because Downing lacked architectural training, he depended upon the skills of several people, most especially Davis, a superb draftsman, to translate his rough pencil sketches into finished artwork. Original designs by Davis, such as the Albany, New York, villa Davis designed for J. Rathbone, and The Knoll in Tarrytown, New York, were featured in Downing's books as well.

Downing's *Cottage Residences, or A Series of Designs for Rural Cottages and Cottage-Villas and Their Gardens and Grounds Adapted to North America,* published in 1842, promised "smiling lawns and tasteful cottages." It featured Tuscan designs and those adapted from rural English Gothic cottages. The Tuscan or Italian style was considered to be more appropriate for tropical climates, while Rural Gothic to be more fitting for homes located in an area with changing seasons. Davis and Downing envisioned the cottage as ideally suited for small working-class families. Frequently symmetrical, it was characterized by board-and-batten siding, a steeply pitched gable trimmed with carved vergeboards, pinnacles, clustered chimney stacks, hood moldings, windows in the form of pointed lancets, oriels, and bays, and last, but far from least, front verandas. "The veranda became for Davis a major architectural component," observed William Pierson, Jr., "and in the end would be a mark of distinction between the American and English houses of the Gothic Revival. . . . Although the porch was not new to American architecture, the idea that the veranda was the link between the house and nature had picturesque connotations that had not been encountered before."[5]

One of the distinctions Downing made between cottages and villas was that, for cottage dwellers, household duties were performed by family members or one domestic while the villa needed three or more servants to run. Unlike that of cottages, the interior space of a villa was asymmetrical. Downing defined a villa as a country residence characterized by irregularity, with part of its surround-

A hand-colored lithograph from Alexander Jackson Davis's Rural Residences shows a charming rustic cottage designed as a gate lodge at Blithewood in Fishkill, New York. Davis, in his description of it, called attention to its rustic porch, bay and mullioned windows, high gables with ornamental carved vergeboards, and chimney shafts.

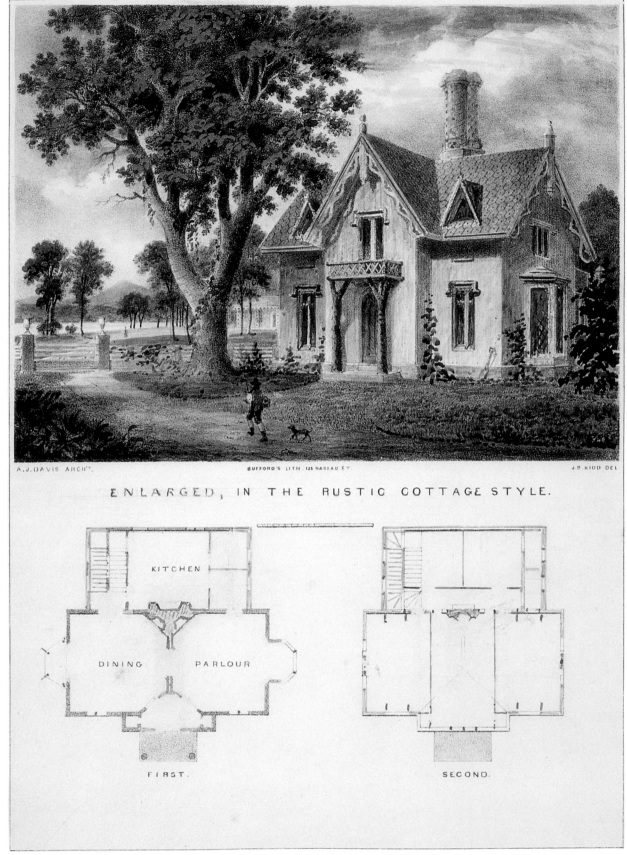

A.J. DAVIS ARCH'T.   BUFFORD'S LITH. 125 NASSAU ST.   J.B. KIDD DEL.

ENLARGED, IN THE RUSTIC COTTAGE STYLE.

KITCHEN

DINING   PARLOUR

FIRST.

SECOND.

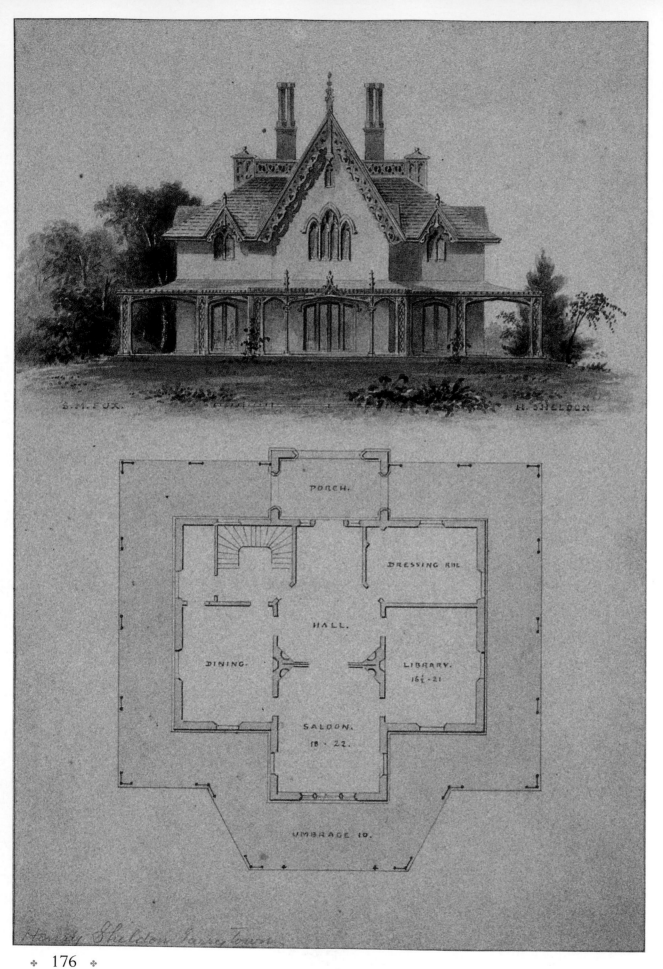

Millbrook, the late-1830s residence of Henry Sheldon, located in Tarrytown, New York, is the work of A. J. Davis. Illustrated in Downing's Treatise on Landscape Gardening, it presented the architect's vision of the appropriate American cottage and bears a strong similarity to Davis's design for the Rotch House.

ing land "laid out as a pleasure ground. Its owner should be a man of some wealth . . . and taste."[6]

Downing, whose houses were frequently simplified versions of those found in English architectural books with a veranda added, was greatly influenced by English Gothic advocates A. W. N. Pugin, writer and critic John Ruskin, and John Claudius Loudon, horticulturist and celebrated author. Loudon, credited with popularizing the adoption of a romantic garden and picturesque landscape for the less well-to-do in England, wrote several successful encyclopedias on such topics as gardening, architecture, and furniture, which Downing did not hesitate to borrow from with great frequency. Downing, in fact, edited Loudon's books for the U.S. market, helping to popularize them through editorials in the *Horticulturist,* a monthly journal of which he was editor. Downing's essays featured in the *Horticulturist,* on subjects ranging from landscape gardening to rural architecture, were compiled and issued in *Rural Essays* a year after his death.

In 1850 Downing published *The Architecture of Country Houses,* the most popular of his architectural books. In it he wrote, "Those who love shadow and the sentiment of antiquity and repose will find pleasure in the quiet tone which prevails in the Gothic style."[7] Downing dropped landscaping in this publication, concentrating on architecture, interiors, and furniture as well as heating and ventilation. The following year Downing was invited to submit a landscaping design for the grounds surrounding the Capitol building, the White House, and the Smithsonian, but only a small portion of his plan was ever carried out. During this time he traveled along the East Coast, giving advice on laying out grounds and siting houses for twenty dollars a day, but referred all architectural design requests to Davis.

Downing had suggested to Davis in 1848 that they turn their informal collaboration into a closer alliance, but Davis appeared uninterested. Two years later, Downing journeyed to England in search of a suitable partner and returned with twenty-six-year-old Calvert Vaux. They worked together for two years before Downing's untimely death on July 28, 1852, three months short of his thirty-seventh birthday. While he was traveling on the Hudson River on a steamship, then a common means of transportation, a fire broke out. Downing saved his wife but drowned trying to rescue another passenger.

Vaux remained in the United States, going into partnership with Frederick Law Olmsted and publishing *Villas and Cottages* three years after Downing's death. Dedicated to Caroline Downing and the memory of her husband, it included 370 engravings and reflected the less romantic direction the team had started to take under Vaux's influence. The preface reads: "In this collection of studies there are many marked 'D. & V.' that have a special interest as the latest over which the genial influence of the lamented Downing was exercised. Several of the plans were in progress when the tidings of his sudden and shocking death were mournfully received by his family and friends, and almost as mournfully by thousands, who, knowing him only through his books, still felt that he was to them a dear and intimate companion."[8]

While tastes veered toward High Victorian Gothic following the Civil War, resulting in dwindling commissions for Davis, who died in 1892, he and Downing's collaborated influence in the middle years of the nineteenth century was profound. Freely experimenting with flexible new forms, their architecture reflected the vitality and idealism of the young nation, contributing greatly to the architectural heritage of America. Their timing could not have been better as an expanding economy created an exploding market for new homes.

Rotch House

Above and opposite: The Rotch House, one of architect A. J. Davis's most endearing houses, is a celebration of the American Gothic style, with its extended central gable, oriel window, and tall chimneys. Downing believed that no dwelling was complete without a porch or veranda. The veranda, which intersects the entrance front, provides a strong horizontal element. Its lattice-patterned supports reflect the diamond-paned windows throughout the house.

ONE OF THE FINEST examples of the picturesque cottage style is Alexander Jackson Davis's charming Pointed Cottage in New Bedford, Massachusetts, designed for William J. Rotch. Featured in Andrew Jackson Downing's book *The Architecture of Country Houses* with an illustration entitled "The Cottage-Villa in the Rural Gothic Style," it is typical of Davis's cottage form, with its symmetrical massing and extended central gable, although larger in scale than most cottages.

William J. Rotch, the mayor of the thriving mill town of New Bedford, Massachusetts, and a Quaker, was taken with the Gothic style after coming upon a number of examples while honeymooning along the Hudson

River, and in 1845 commissioned Davis to design a Gothic cottage. Davis apparently adapted a rendering he had previously done in 1838, changing the rough stone to dressed stone. Ultimately, however, flush boarding painted the color of stone was used, probably because it was less expensive. The house, set in a pear orchard, was built at an estimated cost of $6,000. The first Gothic Revival house in New Bedford, it made Rotch's sanctimonious grandfather, ensconced in a large Greek Revival house in the same town, upset that his grandson would build in such an outlandish style.

Davis's dramatic use of animated architectural elements, coupled with the house's pared-down ornamentation, is an expression of American Gothic at its best. The veranda, so typical of Davis's designs, intersects the entrance porch, its latticed supports repeating the pattern of the diamond-paned windows. Downing's description calls attention to the aspiring lines of the roof and the horizontal lines of the veranda, stating that the house's dramatic high-pointed gable "would be out of keeping with the cottage-like modesty of the drooping, hipped roof, were it not for the equally bold manner in which the chimney-tops spring upwards."[9]

Some time later, Rotch built an addition to the house for his family of nine children. About that time, dormers were added to the front to let in light to the third story. Chimneys flanking the central gable, which were originally clustered with terra-cotta chimney pots, were rebuilt, perhaps because of structural problems. Around World War I, the addition was removed (it is now a free-standing house just behind) and the main house was moved back about fifty feet. Interestingly, the house now to the south side was designed by Davis as well.

Beautifully preserved, the Rotch house is still in the hands of its original family. The present owner, John Bullard, a descendant who, coincidentally, has also served as mayor of New Bedford, moved into the house with his family in the mid-1970s. In 1980, the house was struck by lightning while the Bullards were away. The ensuing fire destroyed the roof, the third floor, and a portion of the second. Water damage was considerable as well. Since then, the Bullards, who have a special feeling for their home and a strong sense of tradition, have painstakingly restored their treasured house, recognizing its historical significance as a living monument to Davis and the American Gothic Revival.

The Rotch House, nearly square, is planned around a central hall. Architectural features, such as side bay windows in the living and dining rooms, bring a liveliness to the interior spaces.

The vergeboard edging the extended central gable, with its intersecting large finial, is made up of fluid scallops tipped with fleurs-de-lis. From the center pointed window, with its tiny balcony, and from the oriel window below, the harbor of New Bedford can be seen.

Lyndhurst

Lyndhurst, the finest Gothic Revival mansion in the United States, is set in the midst of a hundred-acre estate outside Tarrytown, New York, on a bank of the Hudson River. The view opposite looks west toward the front of the villa. First built in 1838 for William Paulding and called The Knoll, Lyndhurst was enlarged in 1864 by architect A. J. Davis, who was responsible for its original design.

Above: A detail of Lyndhurst's front (east) façade shows an oriel window that was part of the original structure. Its finial is repeated at the peak of the roofline, which was raised during the 1864 renovation. The crenellated edge of the veranda can be seen below.

WHILE COTTAGES were extremely popular in the United States through the 1840s and early 1850s, castellated villas were rare. Alexander Jackson Davis introduced the concept to the Hudson River Valley near New York City, designing baronial castles such as Ericstan and the Herrick House in 1855. But it was Lyndhurst, the finest surviving Gothic mansion in the United States today, that was Davis's masterpiece and the first of many Gothic villas to be built along the banks of the scenic Hudson River, an area rich in American history.

Formed by glaciers and fed by northern Adirondack lakes, the Hudson River and its valley boasts landscapes of great variety and beauty. Henry Hudson, for whom the river was named, explored the river in his search

for the Northwest Passage to China. The Algonquin Indians once lived and traded along its banks; Washington's men pitched their camp along its shore. Three-quarters of a century later, the banks of the Hudson were looked upon as an ideal picturesque setting for the castles of rich industrialists. Wealthy New Yorkers, drawn to its beauty as well as its accessibility to the city, began building sizable country estates in its valley.

The Knoll, as Lyndhurst was first called, sits on a bold promontory high above the Hudson River. It was built in 1838 by General William Paulding, once mayor of New York City. Seventy-year-old Paulding, from one of the most prestigious New York families, had commissioned Ithiel Town and Alexander Jackson Davis to execute the design of his house. Davis, who loved the majestic Hudson and the untamed beauty of its valley, created a quintessential Gothic villa, complete with turrets, bay windows, buttresses, trefoils, finials, and crenellations, inspired by Lowther Castle in England. Of pale gray Sing Sing marble, it was surrounded by naturalistic grounds that included stables, gatehouses, and a greenhouse.

In 1864 The Knoll was sold to George Merritt, a prominent New York merchant, who renamed it Lyndhurst. Merritt needed a larger house to accommodate his family and had the good sense to engage Davis, now in his prime and with a sizable collection of Gothic buildings to his credit, to design an addition. Davis skillfully expanded his initial design to double the space. The house's original form was retained as additions were harmoniously incorporated, controlling the scale and keeping the house from becoming overwhelming. Davis skillfully utilized light, shadow, and texture, blending beautiful detailing with a great variety of shapes to form a unified structure. Originally symmetrical, Lyndhurst became decidedly asymmetrical, with its new wing, tower, and bay windows creating a house that was revolutionary in its freely developed interiors.

Jay Gould became Lyndhurst's third owner, purchasing it in 1881. A powerful business magnate who then controlled the Western Union Telegraph and the New York Elevated, he made few changes to the house. Gould's daughter inherited Lyndhurst upon his death, and when she died in 1964, she left the estate to the National Trust for Historic Preservation. Lyndhurst is now open to the public throughout the year.

Lyndhurst's broad veranda, an essential part of the original plan, initially wrapped around the west and south sides of the house, seen here. Later, it was extended to the front east side. Its strong vertical line unified the new additions.

During remodeling, the original porte cochère was enclosed in glass and transformed into a vestibule with a veranda extending from either side. A new single-story turreted porte cochère was built in front of it.

The first greenhouse was built on the Lyndhurst estate about 1870 by George Merritt. It was wonderfully fanciful, with an enormous onion-dome top.

Opposite: Hexagonal bays extend from both ends of the dining room. Composed of three pairs of floor-to-ceiling windows with painted glass, their frames duplicate the ornate tracery around the walls. Niches with Gothic arches, displaying sculpture, fill the corners of the room.

Lyndhurst's elaborate dining room, located in the newer north wing, was large enough to entertain in a grand manner. Clustered columns around the glazed and stenciled walls were painted to duplicate the marble of the fireplace.

A silver and brass wall sconce, one of a pair flanking the dining room bay window, was originally made with gas jets. Now adapted to electricity, it is believed to be from the early twentieth century.

This long hallway leads from the entrance hall, with its faux stone walls, to the dining room. On the right is one of a pair of beautiful Gothic chairs designed by Davis, inspired by rose windows in Gothic cathedrals.

One of over fifty pieces of furniture designed by Davis for Lyndhurst, this oak hall chair from about 1840 is ornamented with cusps, Gothic arches, and a leaf finial top; its octagonal legs end in foliate feet.

Opposite: A small jewel of a room, the master bedroom at the south end of the corridor, with its lovely vaulted ceiling, was enjoyed by all of its owners. A Gothic bed designed by Davis is tucked into the left corner.

On the second floor, just across from the picture gallery, a large bedroom reserved for guests is dominated by a magnificent Gothic window with a small triangular inset filled with Tiffany glass above it.

The guest bedroom has a painted and stenciled Tudoresque ceiling, part of which is shown in this detail. The master bedroom is considerably smaller, reflecting the nineteenth-century practice of saving the best for guests.

Part VI

The Flowering of American Gothic

SPIRIT OF ROMANTICISM pervaded the American scene at the beginning of the nineteenth century, setting the stage for the eventual acceptance of Gothic in the United States. This decidedly romantic mood was articulated in the middle decades of the century by American philosophers Henry David Thoreau and Ralph Waldo Emerson, who encouraged a return to a simple life governed by nature. It was also beautifully illuminated in the work of landscape artists of the time, whose paintings were a clear reflection of the nation's reverence for nature and optimism in a land full of boundless promise. Attitudes concerning the American wilderness, earlier viewed by pioneers in terms of hardships endured during exploration, had undergone a major change. Joined by a fierce new patriotism that emerged after the War of 1812, artists began celebrating the simplicity and beauty of the distinctive American landscape.

Around 1825, the nation's first native school of landscape painting appeared; made up of an unorganized group of about fifty artists who shared a similar style and an understanding for the land, it became known as the Hudson River School. At its head was Thomas Cole, whose naturalistic views of the Hudson attracted local artists such as Asher Durand, Frederic E. Church, John Kensett, and George Inness. Their art, celebrating nature in all its aspects, possessed a sense of innocence and an idealized grandeur. Romanticized visions of the Hudson and the Catskill mountains

Louisiana's Old State Capitol in Baton Rouge, situated on a high bank overlooking the Mississippi River, was designed by James Dakon, a one-time partner of A. J. Davis, and built in 1849. Mark Twain, disapproving of its Gothic facade, referred to it as a sham castle in his Life on the Mississippi. The dramatic Gothic interior of the castellated building has recently been restored to the 1880 period and converted to a state museum.

were commonly executed in sweeping panoramic views. To a large degree, European perception of the United States was based on the art of these Hudson River painters. The Hudson River served not only as a stimulus to the imagination of artists but its banks also proved to be an appropriate background for Gothic architecture. While the rough northern areas were better suited to the castle-like villas, it was the southern region, with its picturesque views of the Palisades and its closeness to New York City, where many wealthy New Yorkers chose to build.

By the middle of the nineteenth century, the American landscape abounded with a variety of Gothic structures, from theaters right down to dog houses. Gothic turned up in cities and towns across the country, adopted for schools—such as Kenyon

College in Gambier, Ohio; the United States Military Academy at West Point; and Virginia Military Institute—and for municipal buildings, like the Town Hall in Northampton, Massachusetts, and the Old Louisiana State Capitol in Baton Rouge, designed by James Dakon, a one-time partner of A. J. Davis. Mark Twain, who as writer Wayne Andrews observed, "would one day come down with the Gothic contagion himself," wrote, "Sir Walter Scott is probably responsible for the capitol building for it is not conceivable that this little sham castle would ever have been built, if he had not run the people mad, a couple of generations ago, with his medieval romances."[1]

Prisons, like the castellated Eastern Penitentiary in Philadelphia; cemeteries, like Crown Hill in Indianapolis; and train depots, like Church Street Station in Nashville, were undeniably Gothic. So were

San Francisco's Engine Company number 15 and Baltimore's Engine House number 6, as well as Chicago's 1869 Water Tower, which managed to survive the Great Fire of 1871. Even bridges, from a small one in New York City's Central Park to the fanciful Philadelphia Chestnut Street Bridge, were not immune. By mid-century, Gothic designs were being made up in cast iron and applied to a vast assortment of commercial buildings as well.

It was a time of economic prosperity and expansion westward, aided by a growing network of railroads; it was also a time of great achievements

The imposing Green-Wood Cemetery entrance and gatehouse, built in 1861 in Brooklyn, New York, of Belleville brownstone, was designed by Richard Upjohn and his son Richard Mitchell Upjohn. Its elaborate Gothic arches recall façades of monumental Gothic cathedrals.

Philadelphia's Chestnut Street Bridge, which once spanned the Schuylkill River, is shown shortly after a 1902 flood. The cast-iron bridge, built in 1861–66 with Gothic arcade and decorative quatrefoils, was designed and engineered by Strickland Kneass. Considered one of the most handsome bridges in the country, it was demolished in 1958.

heralding remarkable inventions and social changes. An emerging middle class with the desire as well as the means for a home of their own brought about a building boom, which became the most progressive period for residential construction America has ever seen.

Country houses were becoming larger, with more elaborate ornamentation, frequently including ribbed and vaulted ceilings, carved mantels and paneling, and stained-glass windows. It was fashionable for houses to have at least one Gothic room; where other styles dominated, libraries were often decorated in Gothic motifs. Houses that took the whole plunge into Gothic possessed not only a sense of drama but a respect for their sites as well; picturesque yet practical, these homes ranged from castellated small fortresses to the gingerbread confections referred to as Carpenter's Gothic.

Carpenter's Gothic architecture, distinguished by the use of sawn and carved ornamentation, was a phenomenon unique to the United States, which had a rich tradition in carpentry, and became so popular that it evolved into a vernacular form. As Gothic flowered in rural and urban settings across the American landscape, lively interpretations were encouraged by the development of the steam-powered scroll saw, a woodworking tool readily accessible by the 1830s, providing American craftsmen with the means to execute endless varieties of intricate designs. The carved-wood decoration known as gingerbread, a term first used in eighteenth-century England to describe fancy carved decoration on a sailing ship, was actually an imitation of stone tracery found in medieval Gothic buildings. Like original Gothic forms, the roots of its ornamentation were often to be found in nature.

At first, decoration was applied to traditional shapes. Generally, earlier houses were remodeled with classical and Gothic features combined. Perhaps the best example of this is what is known as the Wedding Cake House in Kennebunk Landing, Maine. The addition of a Gothic barn to the prop-

Design XXV.

Pl. CI.

Sam.l Sloan Arch.t

P.S.Duval & Co's Steam lith.Press,Phil.a

A GOTHIC FRONT.

Left and opposite: Samuel Sloan, a prominent Philadelphia architect, published a highly successful two-volume folio-sized pattern book entitled The Model Architect *in 1852. Plates included a selection of housing from modest to mansion, as well as details such as those shown here for a veranda post and bracket, gable, window, and balcony rails for a rustic wayside cottage.*

erty encouraged its owner, George Bourne, to build an exuberant lace shell of woodworking superimposed over the surface of his Federal house in 1855, producing, through an uninhibited addition of elaborate pinnacles, boarded buttresses, crenellations, and spandrels, a uniquely personal dwelling.

Architectural handbooks and builder's manuals became quite popular as a number of American writers followed Andrew Jackson Downing's lead by bringing out pattern books featuring Gothic designs. Samuel Sloan, whose best-selling *The Model Architect* was presented in two folio-sized editions in 1852 and 1853, also published *Architectural Review and Builders Journal,* the first professional journal on its subject, from 1868 to 1870. William Roulett's

The Architect (1847), Lewis Allen's *Rural Architecture* (1852), Gervase Wheeler's *Rural Homes* (1853) and *Homes for the People in Suburb and Country* (1855), plus George Woodard's nine books and Arnot's *Gothic Architecture Applied to Modern Residences,* were all eagerly read by a surge of new homeowners.

While local craftsmen referred to pattern books, copying decorative designs from them, or chose from a variety of decorative Gothic trims available from lumber mills, by the late 1830s free interpretations flourished; imaginative renderings created great diversity, ranging from primitive to the highly sophisticated. "The opportunity of decking verandas, gables and eaves with 'gingerbread' stimulated a vernacular expression of folk art that blossomed in the invention of a great variety of fanciful creations,"[2] asserted Jane B. Davies in her introduction to the catalogue for the Houston Museum of Fine Art's 1976 exhibition on American Gothic.

While far removed from medieval cathedrals in appearance, nineteenth-century Gothic cottages and villas shared with them the element of verticality. Pointed arches and windows, towers, extended gables ornamented with finials and pendants, tall clustered chimney stacks (English writer John Claudius Loudon believed that "in every human dwelling these [chimney pots] ought to be conspicuous objects, because they are its essential characteristics"[3]), and board-and-batten siding all pointed skyward, creating a strong vertical illusion. Board-and-batten siding, often utilized by Davis in his cottage designs, consisted of a narrow strip of wood nailed over the joint formed by the meeting of two wider vertical boards. Downing agreed, finding it to be an expression of strength and more truthful than the horizontal clapboard used in Colonial houses. It was one of the architectural elements that distinguished American Gothic cottages from their English counterparts.

There were numerous other distinctive characteristics of American Gothic architecture that accounted for its great diversity. These included carved vergeboards decorating gables and dormers; hood moldings; verandas with decorative supports, spandrels, and crestings; crenellations along rooflines; and a wide variety of windows, from narrow lancets to diamond-paned casements occasionally sporting tracery and stained glass, as well as projecting bay and oriel windows.

The popularity of Gothic varied from one region to another. Two fine examples in the West are the Lace House, located in the mining town of Black Hawk, Colorado, and General Mariano Vallejo's Lachryme Montis (Tear of the Mountain) in Sonoma, California. The Mexican general, a cultured man, purchased three prefabricated Carpenter's Gothic cottages that had been shipped from the East around Cape Horn after the acquisition of California in 1850 to show his patriotism for his new coun-

try. Besides Lachryme Montis, one was constructed in San Francisco and lost in the great earthquake, and the other was constructed in Benecia for one of Vallejo's daughters.

Gothic failed to make major inroads in the South because of an absence of major industry, yet scattered examples can be found. While plantation owners on the whole preferred Greek Revival, certain Louisiana plantations—such as the highly decorative Afton Villa, which was destroyed by fire in 1963, and the Orange Grove plantation—as well as Errolton, a typical antebellum house in Mississippi with Gothic columns and arches, strayed from the norm. The first James River plantation house to be built in the Gothic taste was Belmead, the work of A. J. Davis, currently in need of major repair.

An interesting incarnation of Carpenter's Gothic architecture appeared at religious campgrounds, a phenomenon that manifested itself during the first half of the nineteenth century. Religious freedom guaranteed by the young American democracy spawned a wave of religious fervor that proved to be fertile soil for numerous new Christian religious sects, all actively vying for members. Revivalist and camp meetings, which sprang up all over the country, were among the more successful ways to achieve conversion. These gatherings, lasting from several days up to a week, were unique to the United States.

Thousands of eager participants flocked to designated locations to hear evangelistic sermons delivered by itinerant preachers and, in the heat of the emotion, experienced conversion amid shouting, shaking, and falling to the ground in a state of mild hysteria. Meetings offered an occasion to participate in animated devotion, setting aside worldly affairs for spiritual renewal; they also presented an opportunity for socializing. Open-air revival meetings on the western frontier brought together isolated settlers, scattered throughout remote areas, who welcomed an opportunity for companionship. In the South, meetings were held in September after harvesting; farmers would often arrive with cows in tow in need of daily milking. Camp gatherings in the East tended to attract people from urban areas, who journeyed to a rustic country setting as much for the chance to experience the simple pleasures of nature as to experience religious enlightenment.

Presbyterians were the first to undertake these outdoor meetings, but they were shortly joined by Baptists and Methodists, two of the fastest-growing denominations between 1800 and 1850. Methodist camp meeting sites sprang up around the country, yet they were never formally recognized by the Methodist Church because of their emotional and sometimes controversial nature, and the church's archives contain no mention of their existence. One of the most successful Methodist camp meeting sites, and the largest of eight in Massachusetts, was Wesleyan Grove, later known as Oak Bluffs. Now a seaside community on Martha's Vineyard, it is filled with some of the country's best-preserved Carpenter's Gothic houses.

What began in 1835 as a small gathering of nine tents in the woods eventually evolved into a permanent community with the introduction of campground cottages. One summer Sunday in 1858, twelve thousand people journeyed to Oak Bluffs to attend a service preached by a hundred clergy. It was during the 1850s that A-frame canvas tents started being replaced by campground cottages, an architectural form new to America. Many sported exuberant gingerbread carvings on gables, doorways, windows, and balconies, sometimes combining a number of patterns.

Shelter Island Grove, a later and smaller camp meeting site located just off the tip of Long Island, New York, is another thriving summer community

An American transferware platter from about 1850 ornamented with a Gothick pavilion in its center. More typically brown or blue with white, the mauve shown here is less common.

A rosewood hall chair about four feet high was made in New York City by Alexander Roux and dated 1850. Its seat lifts up for storage.

A mahogany side chair from a set of twelve was made in New York City about 1860.

boasting a selection of charming Carpenter's Gothic houses. Boston landscape architect Robert Morris Copeland, who had laid out the streets, parks, and lots in an area bordering Wesleyan Grove, Massachusetts, was responsible for the campground layout. In 1871 a group of Methodist churchmen from Brooklyn, New York, headed by John French, who had ties to Wesleyan Grove, purchased three acres in an area of Shelter Island then known as Prospect. The following year the Shelter Island Grove Camp Meeting Association was formed and five cottages were built. By 1883, the number of cottages had climbed to two hundred. The small community, now known as Shelter Island Heights, has remained virtually unchanged since its inception save for the loss of the 1873 Prospect Hotel, which functioned as the social center of the community and which burned down in 1942.

By the middle of the nineteenth century, Gothic motifs began appearing on all manner of household objects made in America, finding their way to furniture and decorative accessories, dinnerware, fabric and wallpaper, stoves, lighting fixtures, and a great variety of other articles. Gothic furniture was especially fashionable for libraries and halls. The best Gothic furniture was designed for specific houses by respected architects. Davis designed furniture for all his important houses, creating fifty Gothic designs for Lyndhurst.

With the end of the Civil War in 1865, the country was left disillusioned. The American dream, encouraged by economic development brought on by expanding industrialization, had turned from a fascination with nature to the desire to conquer it. In a time of great economic growth and exploitation, Americans soon began to amass huge fortunes and to build impressive houses. Europe beckoned to the nouveau riche, who now turned away from the naïve charms of Hudson River paintings to Impressionism, a new form sweeping Europe. For the lower classes, cities that had sprung up in the wake of the expanding railroad beckoned seductively, bringing a shift away from rural areas to cities and their surrounding suburbs.

Right: This cast-iron andiron made around 1850 is American. Its lively surface and shape recalls Gothic spires. Far right: A delicate side table made in Philadelphia in the 1840s, its base is trimmed with acorn finials.

The Gothic cottage at Andalusia is ornamented with pointed gables, diamond-paned windows topped with hood moldings, and crenellated bay windows.

Andalusia

One of the few sham ruins in the United States, this charming grotto sits on a bank of the Delaware River among the grounds of Andalusia. Built in 1834, it was originally used as a reading room and a resting spot for ladies strolling the estate grounds.

THIRTEEN MILES north of Philadelphia, a rough-hewn stone grotto in the form of a Gothic ruin sits picturesquely along a bank of the Delaware River. It has been part of a large estate known as Andalusia, the home of the Biddles, a distinguished American family, for close to two centuries. Originally consisting of 113½ acres, the estate was first purchased in 1795 by John Craig, an export trader whose connections with Spain must have influenced his selection of the name Andalusia. Craig's daughter married Nicholas Biddle, a prominent banker who was to become president of the Second Bank of the United States. Upon his wife's parents' death in 1814, Biddle purchased her family's property.

Great care and considerable money went into developing the grounds,

The Gothic pool pavilion at Andalusia, on a broad expanse of lawn to the side of the cottage, is in fact a portion of a porch rescued from a Carpenter's Gothic house along the Hudson River that had been demolished.

which included exquisite gardens and natural woodland. Andalusia was also a working farm, with stables housing some of the country's finest horses. The estate was comprised of cottages, farm buildings, a dairy, and a late Federal style house, which was modernized and extended in 1834 by Thomas Walter, who transformed it into a Greek Revival mansion with a striking white columnated façade.

While the main house was decidedly classical, the spacious grounds abounded with Gothic structures. The grotto at the river's edge, a rare surviving remnant reminiscent of eighteenth-century English sham ruins, was built as a summer house and initially used as a reading room and a resting spot for ladies during their stroll around the gardens. It, too, was designed by Thomas Walter and now serves as a mausoleum, holding the ashes of several members of the Biddle family.

Walter transformed a small farmhouse a few years later at Mrs. Biddle's request into a Gothic cottage, which he included in his book *Cottage and Villa Architecture*. The lighthearted spirit of eighteenth-century Gothic permeates the Gothic cottage. Enlarged in 1853, it is now the private residence of historian James Biddle, who has added to its wonderful assortment of Gothic furniture and accessories. Interior designer George Doan worked with Mr. Biddle to revitalize the cottage interiors in 1976.

Toward the back of the estate is a whimsical Carpenter's Gothic garden house dating from about 1855. Dwarfed by towering trees, it sits in the distance looking like a child's playhouse. It was brought to Andalusia from The Dell, an estate on the Delaware just south of Andalusia. The delightful Gothic Pool Pavilion is a relative newcomer to the grounds, added in 1970. It was actually a portion of a porch salvaged from a Hudson River Carpenter's Gothic house that had been demolished.

The descendants of Nicholas Biddle, who have included bankers, lawyers, diplomats, and senators, have carefully preserved Andalusia. Now, James Biddle, a past president of the National Trust, has set up the Andalusia Foundation, which operates the property. The beautiful main house and grounds are open to the public by appointment.

A tiny Gothic garden cottage nestled under towering evergreens looks more like a child's playhouse. Built in 1855 on a neighboring estate, it is now at home at Andalusia.

This nineteenth-century Gothic umbrella stand of cast iron is situated by the doorway of the front porch. It is one of many Gothic treasures that fill the cottage at Andalusia.

The cottage entrance hall is reminiscent of Strawberry Hill, with its trompe l'œil tracery wallpaper. The Gothic oak bench and chair, both American, are original to the house. The pedestal holding an English Gothic lamp and the radiator cover carved with Gothic motifs are twentieth-century.

Above: Gothic treasures abound throughout the cottage. Here in one of two sitting rooms, a lovely Gothic open oak armchair original to the house, on the left, is joined by one of American mahogany from about 1840. The decorative carved pelmet and bookcase are recent additions.

A diamond-paned bay window in a back room, which serves as an office for owner James Biddle, holds a hexagonal Gothic pedestal table of mahogany. It is accompanied by a pair of maple American Gothic chairs original to the house.

Opposite: The master bedroom is dominated by a beautifully carved Gothic bed painted to look like maple. It was a gift from Joseph Bonaparte, the brother of Napoleon, to Nicholas Biddle about 1833. The Gothic painted pine side table is English.

The warm tones of the dining room walls provide a pleasing background for the beautiful squared-back English Gothic chairs in mahogany from about 1815. Both the center table and a small round one in the extending bay are twentieth-century interpretations.

One of the cottage's treasures is this delightful American Gothic marble-topped mahogany side table from about 1840. Its apron is ornamented with quatrefoils while its legs are formed by clustered columns. The Gothic table clock on it is French.

Roseland

Right: Built in 1846 as a country retreat for Henry Chandler Bowen, Roseland was designed with a main entrance on the south side. The projecting entrance hall and an extending portico were possibly added in the 1880s.

Opposite: Roseland, a Carpenter's Gothic house in Woodstock, Connecticut, is distinguished by an abundance of Gothic motifs, such as board-and-batten siding, triple gables ornamented with vergeboards, pinnacles, and crockets, and decorative chimney stacks of glazed stoneware.

ROSELAND, a picturesque Gothic country retreat built in 1846 for Henry Chandler Bowen, is situated on a green surrounded by prim Colonial homes in a typical New England village. It was the work of English-born architect Joseph Wells, who was better known for the design of Gothic churches.

Bowen, whose main residence was in Brooklyn, New York, chose Woodstock, Connecticut, where he had grown up, to build his country cottage. A successful silk merchant, Bowen published an influential weekly journal called the *Independent* and was a founder of Brooklyn's Plymouth Church. A man of unquestionable virtue, Bowen had selected the "pointed style" of architecture, as Gothic was referred to, because he believed,

as many in the nineteenth century did, that it was morally more appropriate than other architectural styles.

The property was christened Roseland for its flourishing rose gardens set among attractive landscaped grounds, which included a barn with a bowling alley (one of the earliest), an ice house, and a privy. The well-connected Bowen often entertained at his country residence and became known for his lavish Independence Day parties, which were attended by leading writers such as Oliver Wendell Holmes and Henry Ward Beecher, and four United States Presidents of the late nineteenth century.

The design of the lively asymmetrical cottage, while reflecting the influence of A. J. Davis, is unique. Made up of a riot of gables and steeply dormered windows trimmed with carved vergeboards, it sports a variety of windows, from trefoil and oriel to a large pointed tracery window on the east side. The façade facing the street is similar to the Rotch House in New Bedford, with its steep central gable, oriel window, and extending pavilion pierced by side verandas. The main entrance on the south side, however, with its three dormers, bay window, and projecting entrance hall with an extending portico, a possible 1880s addition, is distinctly original. The board-and-batten siding, originally a dusty purple, was painted its present pink with darker trim in the 1890s.

Wells completely furnished the house in the Gothic style at the time it was built, designing some of the furnishings with motifs that repeated interior architectural detailing. Thomas Brooks is believed to have designed a number of pieces as well. Many of the original furnishings are still in the house.

Roseland remained in the Bowen family for 124 years. In 1970 it was acquired by the Society for the Preservation of New England Antiquities and is now open to the public during the summer months.

Opposite: The east side of Roseland, facing the street, has a veranda extending from either side of a pavilion. It is dominated by a large paneled window ornamented with tracery. Above is an oriel window and a large finial that intersects the apex of the gable.

This elaborate carved Gothic settee made of black walnut about 1846 is attributed to Thomas Brooks. It is one of the original pieces of furniture purchased by Henry Chandler Bowen for Roseland's double parlor.

Kingscote

Right: Kingscote is an interesting example of the effective use of light and shadow. Its lively front extends, then withdraws, then projects out again in the suggestion of a tower. The entrance, with its decorative canopy, is tucked back in the recess.

Opposite: Kingscote was Newport's first important nineteenth-century summer house. A handsome asymmetrical Gothic cottage, it was built by architect Richard Upjohn in 1841 for George Noble Jones, a wealthy Savannah planter.

NEWPORT, Rhode Island, has been a favorite summering place for wealthy southerners traveling north to escape heat and disease-carrying insects since the early 1700s. By the start of the nineteenth century, however, the town had lost its position as a leading seaport and gone into a steep decline. Nevertheless, southern visitors continued to arrive, staying in small hotels and rented cottages, and in 1839 George Noble Jones, a prosperous Savannah planter, decided to build a summer retreat there. His would be the first important nineteenth-century house constructed in Newport.

Jones purchased a breezy ridgetop lot with views of the harbor and ocean and hired Richard Upjohn to design a cottage, complete with indoor

A range of decorative Gothic details includes crenellation trimming the edge of a bay window, hood moldings atop windows, rooflines edged with fleurs-de-lis, and gables trimmed with an undulating scalloped vergeboard.

plumbing and sleeping apartments for servants. Upjohn was at the time involved in the design of Trinity Church in New York City and had been responsible a few years earlier for Oatlands, a large Gothic house in Maine built for John Gardiner, Jones's father-in-law. However, Gardiner's daughter, Delia, died before Kingscote was built and Jones moved into his summer cottage in 1841 with a new bride in hand.

The handsome asymmetrical house is unassuming, resembling several of A. J. Davis's designs in *Rural Residences*. It encompasses a wide variety of Gothic forms, such as gables, vergeboards, diamond-paned and bay windows, label moldings, and dorm-

ers, as well as a crenellated entrance canopy and a veranda supported by slender clustered columns. The exterior surface, originally pale beige, is composed of horizontal wooden boards covered with a paint-and-sand mixture and scored to resemble masonry. Its lovely garden, containing a wide variety of native and imported trees, such as paper birch, sweet cherry, Sawara cypress, dogwood, American elm, and balsam fir, reflects the influence of landscape designer A. J. Downing.

Six months after the Civil War broke out, Jones shipped the contents of the house back to Savannah and deeded it to a Canadian relative, motivated, perhaps, by concern that it might be confiscated. In

1863 the cottage was purchased by William King, but several years later King had a mental breakdown, and it was leased by his nephew, David King, Jr., who named it Kingscote. By 1880, Newport had become the height of fashion, with entertaining done in a grand style. King was in need of more space and engaged McKim, Mead & White to design a three-story addition. The architects endeavored to make the addition's exterior, while not Gothic, correspond as closely as possible to the original cottage.

After William King's death, David's widow purchased the house. It ultimately passed on to her granddaughter, Gwendolin Rives, who battled land developers and the city of Newport, who were both intent on destroying the house. Upon her death in 1972, Kingscote was left to the Preservation Society of Newport County and is now open to the public.

A veranda runs along the east side of Kingscote, overlooking grounds filled with an impressive array of trees and shrubs. The house and its landscape reflect A. J. Downing's belief in the importance of siting.

Staunton Hill

Opposite: The picturesque castle-like Staunton Hill, decked out with turrets and exaggerated hood moldings, is situated on a remote hilltop in southern Virginia. It was once a plantation house at the center of a thriving 5,000-acre estate.

Above: A short distance to the west of the plantation house is a Gothic cottage, which functioned as a billiard room as well as a plantation office. Its simple façade has an extending entrance porch with pointed door-ways and a triangular window centered above.

IN 1848, the Gothic plantation house Staunton Hill, designed by John E. Johnson, was built on a bank of the Staunton River in Charlotte County, Virginia, for Charles Bruce. Having graduated from Harvard, Bruce embarked on the Grand Tour through Europe and, upon his return, set up his plantation on five thousand acres purchased earlier by his father, James, who was reputed to be the third wealthiest man in early-nineteenth-century America. Producing tobacco, corn, oats, and hay, the plantation required five thousand slaves to operate. In later years, Bruce went on to become a state senator and collected one of the most valuable libraries in the country.

Staunton Hill was more fortunate than many southern plantation houses. While not far from a number of Civil War battles, it survived untouched

The uninterrupted surface of Staunton Hill's west façade is broken by a diamond-paned oriel window positioned high on top. Just below it is a formally arranged garden.

Below: A crenellated veranda with an extended central portico runs across the symmetrical storybook facade of Staunton Hill. A wide expanse of lawn in front drops sharply to the Staunton River and miles of wilderness beyond.

because of its remote location. Positioned on a hill high above the river with an unencumbered view of miles of wilderness stretching out before it, the house is built in the form of a small symmetrical castle, its castellated and turreted silhouette more closely allied to the garden follies that decorated eighteenth-century English landscape gardens than to the American villas of Downing and Davis.

The Gothic-inspired house includes a large traceried window, flanked by turrets, on the third floor overlooking the river. Label moldings trim diamond-paned second-story windows, while crenellation over the front veranda repeats the edging of the roofline. A diminutive Gothic cottage to the side served as a plantation office and a billiard room.

Inside, Gothic motifs include an octagonal entrance hall with a ribbed ceiling and a library with a bay window facing out onto a colonnaded court. Lining the library walls are carved bookcases ornamented with pointed arches and crenellations divided by clustered columns. Gothic details are also scattered about the house in mantels, on plaster moldings, and in the staircase balustrade, composed of Gothic arches.

For a number of years in the early twentieth century, Staunton Hill fell out of the hands of the Bruce family; however, in 1933, David Bruce, Charles's grandson, repurchased 275 acres of the property, updating the house and adding a wing onto the back. Bruce had little time to enjoy it, however, because shortly thereafter he was appointed head of the OSS in Europe, followed by a stint as Undersecretary of State, then a term as U.S. ambassador to China. During his visits to Staunton Hill, he entertained a number of prominent visitors, from Lady Astor to Dean Acheson. The house and grounds are now in the hands of his son, David S. Bruce, who has recently turned the estate into a conference center.

Staunton Hill's octagonal entrance hall is ornamented with four niches holding classical statuary. Three of its doors, which have pointed paneling, are flanked with clustered columns. The front door has colored insets to simulate stained glass.

One wall of the library, which once housed one of America's most important collections, is lined with arched bookcases divided by clustered columns and decorated with trefoils and crenellation. To the rear is a three-paneled bay window with diamond-paned glass.

Double cottages at Oak Bluffs are rare. Surrounded by a small yard, this one is situated on a corner plot just inside one of the campground entrances.

Bishop Gilbert Haven Cottage

Time seems to have stood still inside the campgrounds of Oak Bluffs, a small community of diminutive cottages on Martha's Vineyard that started life in the middle of the nineteenth century as a Methodist camp meeting site. Wesleyan Grove, as the Methodist campground was initially called, includes several cottages that have been joined together. Here, identical Gothic cottages built around 1869 have been combined into one.

OAK BLUFFS, Massachusetts, today is a town of contrasts; hidden just behind an assortment of noisy restaurants and tourist shops is a tranquil campground, once the site of lively religious revival meetings. Here, ornately trimmed minuscule Carpenter's Gothic cottages, about 320 in all, line narrow winding streets, many unpaved. Sandwiched together, they form irregular rows around a central preaching area, with smaller circles at the outer edges of the grounds. Writer William Pierson, Jr., found these tiny jewels to be "one of the most remarkable concentrations of folk architecture anywhere in the country."[4]

Wesleyan Grove, as the campground was originally called when it was

The cottages were constructed on a platform, about a foot off the ground, of single-layer boarding. Windows and doors were cut out and often the spare material was reused to board up the cottage in winter. The first floor had two rooms, the front being the parlor and the back containing a narrow staircase to the second floor.

formed in 1835, was located on a solitary bluff, bordered by a pond and open pasture—an ideal site for revival meetings. At first there were only a few tents accompanied by a preacher's stand and benches set up in the midst of the half-acre grove of oaks, but by 1854, the number of tents had increased to 200. Days were filled with prayer, song, and meditation. In the evenings, as the sound of hymns filled the soft sea air, the camp took on a magical quality, glowing with lanterns in the trees and candlelight illuminating the tents.

By mid-century, tents began being replaced by tiny, uniquely proportioned cottages, most no larger than twelve by twenty feet, with steep gables pitched at 45-degree angles. A typical cottage was a story and a half high, with a living room on the first floor and a bedroom above under the eaves. Siding was originally single-layer random-width vertical tongue-and-groove planks, but in later years a number of the cottages were covered with shingles. After

1880 most owners added front verandas and dormers to increase the living space. Many cottages lacked kitchens (camp meals were eaten at large communal tents), but, by the turn of the century, kitchens and bathrooms had been added to the backs of most dwellings.

In 1860 the Martha's Vineyard Camp Meeting Association was formed; ten years later an immense octagonal wrought-iron tabernacle was constructed. Around this time two land developing companies, the Oak Bluffs Land and Wharf Company and the Vineyard Highlands, began purchasing property bordering Wesleyan Grove, building houses that turned out to be larger versions of the campground

Most of the cottages have been added to, acquiring porches and usually a kitchen in the back. This Oak Bluffs cottage, with its small overhanging balcony, is one of the few that have not had a roof-covered porch added onto their front.

Opposite below: On either side of a cottage's front door are small lancet windows framed with hood molding. Both windows and doors were cut after the walls were in place. While all the cottages were unique, they possessed a strong similarity that brought a sense of harmony to the storybook community.

cottages. In 1880 the three groups officially united to form the town of Cottage City, renamed Oak Bluffs in 1907. By the turn of the century, there were 500 cottages and 110 tents; with the start of World War I, only one lone tent remained.

One of the more important of the Wesleyan Grove cottages belonged to Bishop Gilbert Haven. The fanciful Gothic cottage, situated on a broad, grassy expanse known as Clinton Avenue, is a prime example of the exuberant camp meeting form of architecture. High gables are trimmed with an undulating carved vergeboard, exaggerated hood moldings end in corbels over windows and doors, and two sets of pointed church-like doors flanked by slender windows, the set above opening to a small overhanging balcony, adorn the front façade. A covered veranda wrapping around on one side was added about twenty years after the cottage was built.

The cottage was originally built in 1872 by Brooklyn resident John French and given to Bishop Haven, an active abolitionist and a preacher at the campground, shortly after he was named a bishop of the Methodist Episcopal Church. A literary man and an admirer of Ruskin, Haven was the editor of the *Zion Herald,* a weekly publication. In August 1874, shortly after Bishop Haven acquired his cottage, President Ulysses S. Grant, accompanied by his wife and an entourage of reporters and friends, visited Wesleyan Grove on a political tour, staying three nights at Bishop Haven's cottage. While the president and his party spent little time on Martha's Vineyard, he and Mrs. Grant attended Sunday services preached by the zealous Bishop Haven, who was reported to have given the greatest sermon of his career.

By 1885, enthusiasm for revivals was all but spent. The camp cottages were now filled with middle-class families who journeyed to the area more for a vacation than for the pursuit of religious enlighten-ment. Today, cottage owners travel from all over the country to open their tiny homes for the brief summer months. The present owners of the Bishop Gilbert Haven cottage, who have owned the cottage for thirty years, come from Ohio to spend each summer in Oak Bluffs. Their four children, all of whom have honeymooned at the cottage, have a special feeling for the time they spent growing up there and now bring their own children to visit and experience the simple pleasures the campground holds.

President Ulysses S. Grant and his entourage are shown here on the porch of Bishop Gilbert Haven's cottage, one of a concentration of Carpenter's Gothic cottages in Oak Bluffs, Massachusetts, a popular nineteenth-century religious camp meeting site.

Bishop Gilbert Haven, a noted orator, received his cottage, one of the larger ones in Oak Bluffs, as a gift from his parishioners shortly before President Grant's arrival.

Above: One of the slender Gothic windows adorning the cottage is inset at the top with colored etched glass, as are many of the cottage windows. The broad hooded molding, with its decorative clover pattern, brings a fanciful touch to the façade. Below: Once on the interior, this decorative Gothic window looking into a small living room was left intact when a kitchen was added to the rear of the cottage enclosing it.

The front porch of the lovely Bishop Gilbert Haven cottage wraps around a side entrance. Its double doors on the ground level and above, flanked with slender pointed windows, repeat the front façade. The porch and its front roof were later additions.

The small
cottage parlor
is simply
furnished.
Interior shutters
add a decorative
element. The
front door is
just to the left.

On a quiet street not far from the harbor at Shelter Island Heights is this Carpenter's Gothic cottage, one of many on this former Methodist camp meeting site.

Tom Fallon Cottage

An ingenious solution for letting in more natural light, the pointed opening, cut high up on one of the stair walls, follows the shape of the cottage's Gothic windows.

HOUSES IN THE METHODIST camp-ground of Shelter Island Grove, situated on the eastern tip of Long Island, New York, were arranged in scallop-shaped rows around the east side of Union Chapel, erected in 1875. While larger than the cottages at Oak Bluffs, many were still modest dwellings. Gothic influences flourished here as well, with an assortment of pointed windows and doors, gabled roofs, and gingerbread trim on the porches, balconies, and towers.

One of the typical Carpenter's Gothic cottages in the quiet community now known as Shelter Island Heights was purchased in 1981 by Tom Fallon as a summer retreat. Built in 1875, it remained in the hands of the Pettit family, the original owners, until about 1960. Initially constructed in the form of a cross, the cottage had undergone a number of changes over the years by the time Mr. Fallon bought it; the dining room and an upstairs bedroom had been extended two and a half feet and the exterior, now covered by weathered shingles, was originally constructed of board-and-batten siding. The spacious living room, which most probably was originally two rooms, included a large rustic stone fireplace as well as wall paneling added at some point after it was built.

Mr. Fallon made a number of changes but believed in the importance of retaining the house's integrity. Since the house was surrounded by deep porches and a thick web of trees and branches, his first priority was to bring light into the house as he set about thinning out the growth. Inside, walls were painted cool shades, and at the top of the stairs,

the upper section of a pointed window, discovered in the basement, was installed under converging eaves, providing a decorative element in one bedroom as well as light to the dark hall. Mr. Fallon added a kitchen by enclosing a portion of the porch.

When it came to decorating, Mr. Fallon, who has a special eye for putting together the unexpected, was assisted by friends who have added to his eclectic collection; each piece that graces this wonderful cottage has a quirky character. As the owner says: "I like to mix up objects with a sense of humor. Wonderful antiques combined with nickel and dime stuff make things come alive." The large living room, with its imposing Gothic chair from a Masonic lodge, as well as the kitchen have an Adirondack feeling to them, while the dining room possesses an eighteenth-century Swedish mood, with its pale

An antique Venetian glass chandelier supplied the inspiration for the peach wall color in the dining room. Combined with the soft tone of the ceiling, it gives the room a Swedish flavor.

The cottage's small guest bedroom has a pointed cutout that not only functions as a charming decorative device but, more importantly, provides light to the stairwell.

The cottage's living room, with its large stone fireplace, a later addition, has the feel of an Adirondack lodge. The cozy low-ceilinged room, filled with an eclectic collection of treasures, is decidedly masculine, with a strong dash of whimsy.

In the far corner of the living room, a finial-topped Gothic chair originally used in a Masonic lodge asserts its presence. The slim shuttered Gothic window looks out to a side porch encircling the cottage.

*Opposite: The pared-
down bedroom in this
fascinating Shelter
Island cottage has great
appeal. Simple in spirit,
it captures a sense of the
original campground
cottage. The double
doors lead to a small
balcony.*

*Ingenuity is the trademark of this cottage kitchen from its butcher
block table made from the sink opening to the built-in dresser
drawers under the rear counter.*

colored walls and its muted aqua ceiling. Mr. Fallon
faux-marbled the floors and added columns. The
dining room's beautiful Venetian chairs were found
in an offbeat antique shop.

Mr. Fallon painted his kitchen floor, then stenciled leaves on it himself. To accommodate a pointed window, found in a junk shop, the ceiling had to
be extended. When the carpenter who built the
kitchen confessed he did not know how to build
drawers, Mr. Fallon found an old dresser and had it
built in under the counter. A butcher-block table is

made from the part of the countertop that was cut
out for the sink opening. The benches are church
pews that were left in the house. Mr. Fallon's goal
was simple: "I wanted a house that would be welcoming, one touched with fantasy that was not to be
taken too seriously." He succeeded admirably.

As a Nation Matures, Gothic Is Transformed

ITH THE END of the devastating Civil War in 1865, newer American architectural styles such as Queen Anne, Stick, and Shingle began usurping the picturesque Gothic so beloved by Davis and Downing. Gothic, however, was not about to be written off. While earlier romantic forms lost favor, the style reemerged under the guise of High Victorian Gothic. This newer form, also referred to as Venetian and Ruskinian Gothic, turned its back on English influences, casting its sights instead on Italy and Germany for design inspiration. Forms remained lively and irregular and buildings became more eclectic and imposing, distinguished by heavy, coarse detailing and polychroming, a method of construction that utilized the intrinsic colors of brick and stone to form contrasting patterns.

Just as Sir Walter Scott sparked an enthusiasm for Gothic in the United States earlier in the nineteenth century, the widely read books of English critic John Ruskin were largely responsible for the creation of this new approach to Gothic. His architectural theories, voiced in two influential books, *The Seven Lamps of Architecture,* published in 1849, followed by his three-volume *The Stones of Venice* in 1851–53, inspired architects on both sides of the Atlantic. "Much of his writing is contradictory (some, in fact, is nonsense)," write Calder Loth and Julius Trousdale Sadler, Jr., in their book *The Only Proper Style,* "but his enthusiasm combined with a gift for

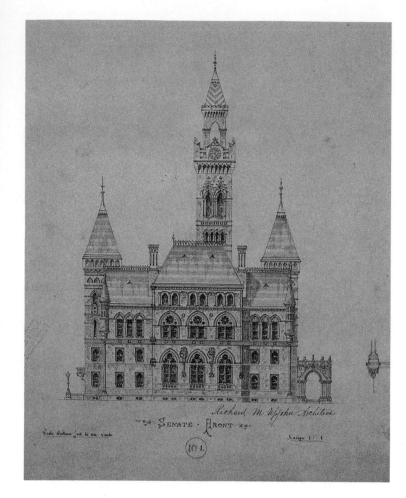

The majesty of government is amply expressed in the High Victorian Gothic Connecticut State Capitol, built in Hartford in 1872–79. The building is the work of Richard Mitchell Upjohn. This ink drawing of the Senate front shows a small portion of the imposing structure.

forceful expression served to make him one of the most popular writers of his time . . . his works remain Victorian classics of the history of taste."[1]

Ruskin's writings are filled with praise for Italian medieval Gothic architecture, with its use of patterns formed by colored masonry and restrained ornamentation so unlike the crockets, pinnacles, and such found in the Gothic forms of Ruskin's native England. He stated in *The Stones of Venice,* "the Veronese Gothic is strong in its masonry, simple in its masses, but perpetual in its variety. The later French Gothic is weak in masonry, broken in mass

and repeats the same idea continually. It is very beautiful but the Italian Gothic is the nobler style."[2]

While Ruskin never went so far as to advocate its actual application, architects became intrigued with his beguiling descriptions and, before long, monumental Venetian Gothic structures started appearing in major American cities throughout the country. Loth and Sadler refer to them as "unabashed declarations of the opulent materialism of a more confident age."[3] Used primarily for commercial structures, such as the city halls in Richmond, Virginia, and Grand Rapids, Michigan, and the Connecticut state capitol in Hartford, the style aptly conveyed the power and majesty of government.

One of the earliest U.S. examples of Ruskinian Gothic was the 1865 National Academy of Art in New York City, where architect Peter Bonnett Wight turned to the Doges Palace in Venice, a favorite of Ruskin's, for inspiration. The Jefferson Market Courthouse, designed by Calvert Vaux in partnership with Frederick Withers, both English transplants, and built in New York in 1875, was one of the most famous of the buildings executed in the High Victorian style. Frank Furness, an American architect particularly adept at this style, was responsible for the 1876 polychromed Pennsylvania Academy of the Fine Arts in Philadelphia, designed with his partner, George Hewitt.

In Boston, the Museum of Fine Arts, completed in 1878, was architect John Sturgis's tribute to High Victorian Gothic, but it only survived thirty years before it was replaced by the Copley Plaza Hotel in 1908. Isabella Stewart Gardiner's Fenway Court, built in Boston in 1901 to house her art collection, was copied from a Venetian palazzo and is now a privately owned museum.

Castle building in the United States was for the most part left to the closing decades of the nineteenth century, when many of the great American fortunes were amassed before the creation of a national income tax. The newly rich, in their need to impress, endeavored to gain social acceptance by flaunting their wealth. They entertained lavishly in ostentatious houses, similar to those owned by European nobility. The construction as well as the maintenance of these opulent estates was facilitated by an influx of immigration at the time, which brought skilled craftsmen as well as unskilled labor into this country.

A number of magnificent homes constructed in the 1880s, a time appropriately referred to as The Gilded Age, were inspired by French châteaux of the sixteenth century, which were a blend of late Gothic and Renaissance influences. American architect Richard Morris Hunt, who had studied and worked in France, was one of the first to recognize a desire among the wealthy for homes that represented their newly found status. He introduced a style referred to as Chateauesque, or Frances I, which was also popular in England among the monied set. While these sumptuous residences mirrored the attitudes of the times, they were to have little influence on more modest dwellings of the common folk. The Vanderbilts were particularly fond of this style; William Vanderbilt built a Hunt-designed New York City mansion at 660 Fifth Avenue in the Chateauesque style in 1881, ornamented with the salamander and crown, the emblem of the French king Francis I. His brother George chose the beautiful Blue Ridge Mountains outside Asheville, North Carolina, as the site for his spectacular mansion. The magnificent Biltmore, situated on a 125,000-acre estate looking out over miles of virgin woodland, was completed in 1895. Still owned by the Vanderbilt family, it is open to the public, who are now able to catch a glimpse of the glittering world of the wealthy around the turn of the century.

The architectural team of Calvert Vaux and Frederick Withers was responsible for the polychromed 1875 Jefferson Market Courthouse at the corner of Sixth Avenue and 10th Street in New York City. One of the most famous of the buildings done in the Ruskinian manner, it once housed a market and a jail.

George Washington Vanderbilt's magnificent Biltmore estate, constructed from 1890 to 1895, is located in Asheville, North Carolina. The eminent architect Richard Morris Hunt was responsible for the Francis I style 255-room mansion. Landscape designer Frederick Law Olmsted laid out the 125,000 acres surrounding the house.

Opposite: Marble House, a sensational Newport mansion built in 1892, has a dazzling Gothic sitting room designed to display small Gothic objets d'art. It is distinguished by stained-glass windows, great bronze chandeliers, and an immense crenellated chimneypiece with panels of domestic scenes.

Left: The most memorable of the rooms at Belcourt, the Newport summer retreat of Oliver Belmont, is the magnificent seventy-foot-long French Gothic ballroom. Five dramatic stained-glass windows depicting early French court life stretch along one wall, with thirteenth-century trefoil windows above them.

This study for the thirty-story Woolworth Building, the Gothic sky-scraper in New York City built in 1913, was done in May of 1910.

Newport, Rhode Island, near the end of the century, became one of America's most prestigious summer resorts. Its rocky seacoast was lined with fabulous mansions set in lush gardens with rare foliage. The mansions were designed for the country's wealthiest and most influential families by leading American architects such as Hunt, Richardson, Codman, and the firm of McKim, Mead & White. Several of the Newport mansions incorporated some form of Gothic, such as an elaborate fireplace at Château-sur-Mer, a French Gothic drawing room in the lavish Louis XIV Marble House of Mr. and Mrs. William Vanderbilt, and a ballroom grand enough to satisfy a medieval king at Belcourt, the Louis XIII hunting lodge of Oliver Belmont.

Chicago had become the center of commerce for the Midwest with the establishment of the railroad system, which transported grain into the thriving city from the prairies for milling and storing and cattle in for slaughter. Its exploding population was to multiply tenfold from 1850 to the great Chicago fire in 1871. The leaders of midwestern society in the 1880s were Mr. and Mrs. Potter Palmer, who were known for their extensive art collection. Their Chicago home, built in 1882 on Lake Shore Drive between Banks and Schiller streets, resembled a medieval Gothic castle. It was the work of architect Henry Ives Cobb. Palmer, a real estate developer and owner of the famed Palmer House, had started his business empire with a dry goods store, which he eventually rented to Marshall Field.

From the ashes of Chicago's destructive fire, which virtually leveled the city, sweeping away tenements, slaughterhouses, factories, and workhouses, emerged a profusion of progressive architectural forms designed by its own breed of architects, such as Louis Sullivan and Frank Lloyd Wright, who established Chicago as a leader in contemporary architecture. The eminent architect Henry Hobson

Richardson was responsible for the 1872 Gothic-style American Express Building, erected in Chicago. It was his first commission and one of the few he did in the Gothic style. Chicago's 1885 Home Insurance Building, the first major structure to utilize steel-skeleton construction, is frequently referred to as the first skyscraper.

The eight-story Venetian Gothic Jayne building, constructed in Philadelphia in 1851, was the first building of some height to be built of iron columns. By the end of the nineteenth century, with the development of cast iron and structural steel, skyscrapers would radically change city skylines, usurping the space that was once the sole domain of spires. Not immune to Gothic influences, these towers of industry and commerce were embellished with historical references linking them to the past, the result of a reluctance to relinquish what was familiar.

Burnham and Root's Masonic Temple, a gabled skyscraper built in 1892, is, in the opinion of respected *New York Times* architecture editor Paul Goldberger, "an icon of turn-of-the-century Chicago."[4] Architect Cass Gilbert turned to Gothic for his 1913 Manhattan masterpiece, the sixty-story Woolworth building, distinguished by its Gothic detailing. The world's tallest building until 1931, it was considered the ultimate in skyscrapers. Three years earlier, the University Club in Chicago, designed by the firm of Holabird and Roche, had been constructed in collegiate Tudor. But the Chicago skyscraper that received the most notoriety was the 1925 Chicago Tribune Tower, a Gothic-inspired steel structure with stone overlay, based on the Tour de Beurre in Rouen, France. It was the result of an intense international design competition sponsored by the *Chicago Tribune,* which was in need of new headquarters and determined to settle for nothing less than the most beautiful building in the world. John Meade Howells and Raymond Hood were its architects.

Collegiate Gothic, frequently selected for a library or chapel, flourished from 1890 to 1930. Colleges such as Bryn Mawr, built near Philadelphia in 1896; Trinity College in Hartford, built in 1873–80; and Yale Harkness Quad in New Haven, built in 1917, emulated such revered English universities as Oxford and Cambridge. The success of collegiate Gothic was due to a considerable degree

This photo of the upper stories of the Woolworth Building highlights its Gothic detailing. The skyscraper, referred to as a cathedral of commerce, looked decidedly to the future while remaining respectful of past traditions.

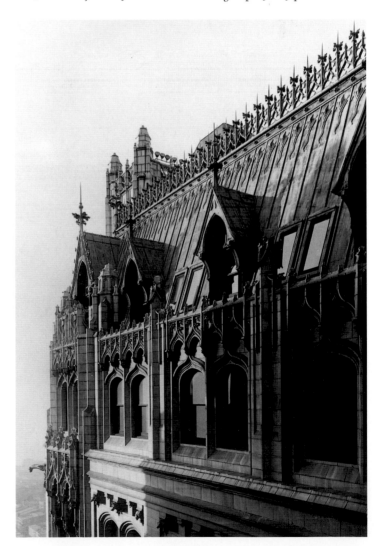

A typical example of the Tudor style popular in the 1920s and early 1930s, this stucco and brick seaside house in New Jersey was built in 1926 by the Mahoney Construction Co. It features a decorative half-timber façade, two cross gables, tall narrow windows, and prominent chimneys.

to leading architect Ralph Adams Cram, who, in partnership with Bertram Goodhue, an outstanding early-twentieth-century draftsman, and Frank Ferguson, until 1914, specialized in ecclesiastic and collegiate structures. Their firm was responsible for the expansion of West Point Military Academy and the University Chapel and Graduate College at Princeton, all designed in the Gothic style.

Cram was a prolific writer and a staunch supporter of Gothic; his *The Gothic Quest,* published in 1907, and *The Substance of Gothic,* published in 1916, were first delivered as lectures. Cram, like Pugin before him, believed that Gothic was the only appropriate style fit for Christian worship, a belief that determined the design of a number of major churches. The group was responsible for the redesign of New York City's St. Thomas Church after fire destroyed Richard Upjohn's original, and at one point they supervised the construction of the recently completed Washington National Cathedral of Sts. Peter and Paul, built in the English Decorated

style of fourteenth-century Gothic—the only great U.S. cathedral to be built in the twentieth century. Cram, Goodhue, and Ferguson received a commission to remodel the immense St. John the Divine in New York City, unfinished to this day, converting it from Romanesque to Gothic.

Gothic turned up in residential buildings during the early decades of the twentieth century in the form of Elizabethan-style manor houses, recognized at the time as a symbol of affluence. By the Roaring Twenties, the automobile offered mobility to many, and, as families moved to the suburbs, medieval-style Tudor houses proliferated. In warmer climates, Gothic appeared with a Venetian or Spanish flavor. One of the more spectacular was Ca'd'Zan, the winter residence of showman John Ringling and his wife, built in Sarasota, Florida, in 1926 and designed by New York architect Dwight James Baum. Gothic forms in general, however, were rapidly losing favor, and in 1928 the respected art historian Sir Kenneth Clark would write that "the real reason

A detail of showman John Ringling's thirty-room Florida mansion, Ca'd' Zan, the exotic Venetian Gothic palazzo, shows its finial-topped ogee-arched doors and windows handmade of tinted Venetian glass. A Gothic observatory tops the sixty-foot Spanish tower, based on a similar tower at the old Madison Square Garden building in New York City.

Ca'd'Zan, on Sarasota Bay, was completed in 1926. Dwight James Baum was responsible for its design, which was based in part on the Doges Palace in Venice. It is constructed of poured concrete and brick with decorative glazed terra-cotta tiles.

why the Gothic Revival has been neglected is that it produced so little on which our eyes can rest without pain."[5]

The Great Depression of 1930 brought a sobering effect to architecture, introducing a profound change. Around 1932, a revolutionary new design movement arrived in the United States. First conceived of in Germany in 1919, the Bauhaus school stripped away ties to the past, concentrating instead on an idealistic, streamlined approach to design. It soon became known in the States as the International Style.

It was not until the 1960s, with renewed interest in restoration and preservation, that a counter-movement surfaced, spearheaded by younger architects like Robert Stern, Robert Venturi, and Charles Moore, who crusaded for the return of ornamentation and architectural references rooted in tradition. This concept of returning to cultural roots revitalized architecture. Tagged "postmodern," it was based not so much on rejecting modernism as on embellishing contemporary forms. Gothic and classical elements that had been languishing for decades once again emerged transformed. Architect Charles Moore commented, "We are all interested in trying to make architecture more interesting by attaching to it images from people's pasts, from people's memories, that make it mean more than the pure forms of the last fifty [or] sixty years."[6]

Many new homes today recall familiar forms, such as the cottage, villa, and meeting house; the most successful combine a respect for past traditions with ingenuity, innovation, and imagination. Neoclassical elements have never been more widely utilized, yet a number of respected architects like Hugh Newell Jacobsen, the Centerbrook Architects, and R. M. Kliment & Frances Halsband have turned to Gothic-related forms, such as extended gables, soaring chimneys, arched windows, and verandas, in their designs for contemporary residences.

Collegiate Gothic interpreted into today's terms is also alive and well. Recent versions include the Lewis Thomas Laboratory for Molecular Biology at Princeton, built in 1986, and the Gordon Wu Hall at Butler's College, Princeton, opened in 1983.

In 1988 the architectural team of Philip Johnson and John Burgee executed a skyscraper at 190 South LaSalle Street in Chicago topped with extended Gothic gables. Gothic strains can be discerned in several other skyscrapers designed by this renowned duo, such as the Atlanta IBM building and PPG Place in Pittsburgh. "The only absolute," Philip Johnson has said, "is that there are no longer any rules, and if this results in a measure of chaos, it also opens up possibilities for inventiveness, just as High Victorian Gothic came as a breath of fresh air after the archaeological correctness of the Gothic Revival."[7]

As we journey into the twilight years of the twentieth century, a distinctly romantic spirit has materialized yet again, motivated in part by an awakened interest in nature and a concern for our environment. With it has come a renewed appreciation for Gothic, with its rich reservoir of motifs and its close ties to nature. As Penelope Hunter-Siebel, in her introduction to the 1989 European Gothic show, "Of Knights and Spires," commented, "We are at last able to cast our eyes on works that were the pride of another age and feel no guilt at the excitement they elicit."[8]

Architecture, in an effort to express the spirit of an age, is constantly being redefined, bringing with it widely divergent attitudes. Yet it is imperative that, whatever the current fashion may be, we not lose sight of the fact that the history of a nation is to be found in the richness of its architectural heritage, created through a layering of a wide assort-

Adorned with trefoils and finials, this
small ogee-arched Gothic conservatory
from the Machin Company, sitting alone
in the landscape, combines the wonders of
modern technology with the spirit of
eighteenth- and nineteenth-century
glass houses.

ment of styles. Much Gothic architecture of value
has been lost through the years because, as it has
gone out of fashion, we have lacked foresight to
preserve it.

Now that Gothic has again emerged out of the
shadows into the limelight, it is hoped that an attempt will be made to save the best remaining examples of it. The time has come to recognize that
Gothic's rich architectural legacy is an important
part of the fabric of America and, as such, should be
regarded as a national treasure.

An oasis of calm, the gracefully arched
glass house is an ideal spot for enjoying
a few quiet moments among a collection
of flowering plants and vines.

Mar-a-Lago

Right: The incredible gold-leaf ceiling is a copy of the Thousand Wing Ceiling in the Accademia in Venice, with sunbursts substituted for angel faces. Painted in the arches is a mille-fleur design accompanied by armorial shields bearing the insignia of the Doges of Venice.

Opposite: Glittering regal lions stand guard at the triple-arched entrance to the splendid salon of Mar-a-Lago, Marjorie Merriweather Post's extravagant Palm Beach mansion, now owned by Donald Trump. Up the sweeping marble stairs, past rows of sinuous columns, a small loggia overlooks the ocean.

THE CONSTRUCTION of the luxurious Royal Poinciana Hotel and the Palm Beach Inn (now the Breakers) around 1894 by Henry M. Flagler, a partner with John D. Rockefeller in Standard Oil, put Palm Beach, Florida, on the map, establishing it as one of the fabled winter watering holes for the rich and famous. In short order, the rich began building lavish homes along its shores. The most sumptuous of these mansions was Mar-a-Lago, owned by Marjorie Merriweather Post, the cereal heiress whose father had established the Postum Cereal Company, which in 1929 became the General Foods Corporation. Ms. Post, who inherited the business in 1914, was instrumental in its phenomenal success.

Marjorie Merriweather Post's fabulous Mar-a-Lago in Palm Beach was completed in 1927. The mansion's salon, the most splendid space in the 115-room house, has rare silk needlework panels from an old Venetian palace inset around the walls.

Marjorie Merriweather Post married four times. Her first marriage, in 1905, when she was eighteen, was to Edward Bennett Close. Edward Francis Hutton, the stockbroker, followed in 1920. Her third husband, Joseph E. Davies, whom she married in 1935 shortly after her divorce, was ambassador to the Soviet Union from 1937 to 1939; her fourth husband was Herbert May, whom she married in 1958. Ms. Post's Washington, D.C., home, Hillwood, is filled with Imperial Russian treasures, many purchased during her stay there. The house was left to the Smithsonian Institution, but in 1978 it was returned to the Marjorie Merriweather Post Foundation and is now operated as a public nonprofit museum open by written request.

With the completion of her Mar-a-Lago winter residence in 1927, Ms. Post became the head of Palm Beach society. Her 115-room mansion, set in seventeen acres of landscaped grounds, took four years to build. The crescent-shaped house, with flanking wings, boasts fifty-eight bedrooms, thirty-three bathrooms, and three bomb shelters. There was also a theater.

The mansion is situated on a coral reef anchored by concrete and steel, with Lake Worth on one side and the Atlantic Ocean on the other. Designed by Joseph Urban and Marion Sims Wyeth, its architecture is a mix of Spanish, Venetian, and Portuguese influences. Old Spanish tiles, some dating back to the fifteenth century, were used extensively inside

The childhood room of actress Dina Merrill, Ms. Post's daughter by her second husband, E. F. Hutton, is out of a fairy tale.
A beehive fireplace is surrounded by a rosebush in plaster relief. A gilded Gothic dressing table is set against one wall.

253

and out. The most important room in the house is the magnificent Italian Gothic living room. Its gold-leaf ceiling is a copy of the Thousand Wing Ceiling in the Accademia in Venice, with sunbursts substituted for angel faces.

Ms. Post died in 1973, leaving her estate, which had been designated a landmark, four years earlier, to the state of Florida, but the state soon found that it was too expensive to maintain, a problem common to these vestiges of an opulent age. Mar-a-Lago, most definitely one of America's architectural treasures, was more fortunate than many. In 1985 it was purchased, along with its furnishings, for ten million dollars by the wealthy developer Donald Trump, who has restored it to its original glory.

The elaborate salon, an opulent fantasy with a sense of a stage set, is Viennese designer Joseph Urban's pièce de résistance. Its focal point is an Italian Gothic hooded fireplace. A pair of Bristol glass chandeliers hang from its spectacular ceiling.

Opposite: Antique Spanish lanterns are suspended from pointed arches around the room, which reflects a blending of Italian, Spanish, Moorish, and Portuguese influences. The entire house displays an amazing concern for detail.

McKim House

Right: The south side of the McKim house is dominated by a long porte cochère leading to the main entrance. It is actually an extension of the roof of a storage shed. A wide cornice with polychromed brackets is tucked under the extending gable of the roof.

Opposite: Sited high on a bluff on Fishers Island, the windswept house has cedar shingles and haphazard rough-hewn stick trim scattered across pediments, brackets, and a balcony. In most houses, windows line up horizontally, giving an indication of where the floors are. Here, they vary in size and placement and are scattered across the exterior, making it difficult to determine where the floors are and how they are placed within a room.

WHEN CHARLOTTE McKIM decided to build a summer retreat, she looked to Fishers Island, where she had spent her summers as a child. This exclusive, little-known enclave located three miles off the Connecticut shoreline in Long Island Sound, accessible only by small plane or boat, has managed to keep an anonymity in an area of the Atlantic Coast where summer brings a flood of tourists.

Ms. McKim, an independent filmmaker and screenwriter, selected Mark Simon and Leonard Wyeth from the architectural firm of Center-brook, headquartered in Essex, Connecticut, to design a house for her that would be informal and would work well when entertaining numerous

Facing north across Long Island Sound, this lively façade has an extended gable window that covers a bedroom balcony and an entrance, one of six, to the dining room below. In front of the dining room is a deck.

weekend guests. Their solution was a structure that redefines Gothic images in twentieth-century terms. Packed with surprises, it forces all who experience it to reevaluate their preconceived notions of space and ornamentation.

The solitary house, positioned on a windswept bluff overlooking the sound, has now settled comfortably into its surroundings. It was constructed in 1988, with a storage shed to one side attached by a roofed walkway. Echoing nearby Gothic Revival houses, it exudes a Gothic feeling in its eccentricity as well as in its use of architectural elements, such as a steep extended roof, gabled and peaked windows, and polychromed brackets running around the wide cornice under the eaves. The gray rough-hewn stick trim that distinguishes the façade is reminiscent of twigwork found in Adirondack cabins, recalling the strong heritage of American craftsmen.

The lively cedar-shingled exterior, with its randomly arranged assortment of pointed windows and its irregular stickwork, which decorates six portes cochères and balcony, hint at the cottage's complex interior. Inside, the four-bedroom house embraces a variety of forms, opening to a round entry that gives way to a hall that in turn leads to an oval living room sited diagonally to the axis of the house and dropped several feet to create extra height. A rectangular dining room, it, too, at an angle, is approached by ascending several steps leading out of the living room. This in turn leads into a square kitchen. The master bedroom, on the second floor, is oval in shape, with a peaked window and small balcony looking out to Long Island Sound and the Connecticut shore beyond. The unexpected mix of shapes and their positioning creates a sense of exploration in a house that refuses to take itself too seriously.

Referred to by editor and writer Martin Filler as "a witty tribute to the eccentric seaside architecture of the late nineteenth century,"[9] this Fishers Island weekend cottage has achieved that delicate balance between playful and functional, reminiscent of the past yet very contemporary.

The large peaked window in the oval master bedroom extends out of the wall as though to form a bay. A small balcony with random stick patterning projects from it. The headboard of the bed repeats the design of the stickwork.

NOTES

Opener.
John Ruskin, *The Stones of Venice* (Boston: Estes and Lauriat, 1851–53), 2:181.

Part I.
1. Horace Walpole, *On Modern Gardening: An Essay by Horace Walpole* (1780; reprint, New York: Young Books, 1931), 38.
2. Kelli Pryor, "Back to Nature," *Avenue Magazine* (February 1989): 133.
3. Walpole, *On Modern Gardening*, 42.
4. Christopher Hussey, *The Picturesque: Studies in a Point of View* (London: Putnam, 1927; reprint, 1967), 130.
5. Lord Kames (Henry Home of Kames), *Elements of Criticism* (Edinburgh: A. Kincaid & J. Bell, 1762), vol. 3.
6. Alexander Pope, essay in *The Guardian* (1713).
7. Horace Walpole to Richard Bentley, September 1753, Correspondence, 35:148, Lewis Walpole Library, Farmington, CT.
8. Rose Macaulay, *Pleasure of Ruins* (London: Weidenfeld and Nicolson, 1953), 27.
9. Walpole to Bentley, Correspondence, 35:148.
10. R. Fish, *The Journal of Horticulture and Cottage Gardener* (1864): 376.
11. Bishop Richard Pococke, *Travels Through England* (Westminster: Camden Society Publications, 1757), 271.
12. Barbara Jones, *Follies and Grottoes* (London: Constable, 1953), 18.

Part II.
1. John Papworth, *Designs for Rural Residences* (London: R. Ackermann, 1818, 1832; reprint, Farnsborough: Gregg International, 1971), 25.
2. Humphrey Repton, *Observations on the Theory and Practice of Landscape Gardening* (London: J. Taylor, 1803), 138.
3. James Chambers, *The English House* (London: W. W. Norton, 1985), 242.
4. Charles Locke Eastlake, *A History of the Gothic Revival* (London: Longmans, Green and Co., 1872; reprint, Leicester and New York: Leicester University Press and Humanities Press, 1970), 43.
5. Kenneth Clark, *The Gothic Revival: An Essay in the History of Taste*, 3rd ed. (New York: Harper & Row, 1962), 94.
6. Quote from *The Statesman* (May 15, 1815), in Christopher

Hussey, "Houghton Lodge—I," *Country Life* (April 10, 1951): 1190.
7. Gwyn Headley and Wim Meulenkamp, *Follies: A National Trust Guide* (London: J. Cape, 1986), 153.

Part III.
1. Jane B. Davies, *The Gothic Revival Style in America, 1830–1870* (Houston: Museum of Fine Arts, 1976), 2.
2. George Eliot, *Scenes of Clerical Life, Mr. Gilfil's Love Story* (New York: Harper & Bros., 1858), 2:354.
3. Terence Davis, *The Gothick Taste* (Rutherford, NJ: Fairleigh Dickinson University Press, 1975), 14.
4. Ibid.
5. Horace Walpole to Henry Seymour Conway, June 8, 1747, Correspondence, 37:269, Lewis Walpole Library, Farmington, CT.
6. Horace Walpole, *A Description of the Villa of Mr. Horace Walpole* (Twickenham, England: Strawberry Hill Press, Printed by Thomas Kirgate, 1784), Preface, iv.
7. From a conversation with Cyrus Redding in c. 1837, quoted in Lewis Melville, *The Life and Letters of William Beckford of Fonthill* (London: William Heinemann, 1910), 299.
8. Linda Hewitt, *Chippendale and All the Rest: A View of English Antiques* (Cranbury, NJ: A. S. Barnes & Co., 1974), 124.
9. Charles Locke Eastlake, *A History of the Gothic Revival* (London: Longmans, Green and Co., 1872; reprint, Leicester and New York: Leicester University Press and Humanities Press, 1970), 44.
10. Davis, *Gothick Taste*, 56.
11. Quoted in Mark Girouard, "Alscot Park, Warwickshire," *Country Life* (May 15, 1958): 1065.

Part IV.
1. Rose Macaulay, *Pleasure of Ruins* (London: Weidenfeld and Nicolson, 1953), 441.
2. Mark Bence-Jones, *Burke's Guide to Country Houses, vol. I, Ireland* (London: Burke's Peerage, 1978), 24.
3. Gavin Stamp and Andre Goulancourt, *The English House 1860–1914* (Boston: Faber and Faber, 1986), 20.
4. Mark Girouard, "Cardiff Castle, Glamorganshire," *Country Life* (April 6, 1961): 760.
5. Olive Cook, *The English House Through Seven Centuries* (Woodstock, NY: Overlook Press, 1983), 293.

Part V.

1. William Pierson, Jr., *American Buildings and Their Architects,* vol. 2, *Technology and the Picturesque: The Corporate and the Early Gothic Styles* (New York: Oxford University Press, 1978), 2:384.

2. Alexander Jackson Davis, *Rural Residences* (New York: the author, 1837, 1838; reprint, New York: DaCapo Press, 1980).

3. Ibid.

4. Ibid.

5. Pierson, Jr., *American Buildings and Their Architects,* 302–3.

6. A. J. Downing, *The Architecture of Country Houses* (New York: D. Appleton, 1850; reprint, New York: Dover Publications, 1969), 388.

7. Ibid.

8. Calvert Vaux, *Villas and Cottages* (1855; reprint, New York: Dover Publications, 1970), x.

9. Downing, 295.

Part VI.

1. Wayne Andrews, *American Gothic: Its Origins, Its Trials, Its Triumphs* (New York: Random House, 1975), 82.

2. Jane B. Davies, *The Gothic Revival Style in America, 1830–1870* (Houston: Museum of Fine Arts, 1976), 6.

3. John Claudius Loudon, *An Encyclopaedia of Cottage, Farm, and Villa Architecture and Furniture* (London: Longman, Brown, Green and Longman, 1833), 15.

4. William Pierson, Jr., *American Buildings and Their Architects,* vol. 2, *Technology and the Picturesque: The Corporate and the Early Gothic Styles* (New York: Oxford University Press, 1978), 2:420.

Part VII.

1. Calder Loth and Julius Trousdale Sadler, Jr., *The Only Proper Style: Gothic Architecture in America* (New York: New York Graphic Society, 1975), 112.

2. John Ruskin, *The Stones of Venice* (Boston: Estes and Laurait, 1851–53), 2:225–26.

3. Loth and Sadler, Jr., *The Only Proper Sytle,* 134.

4. Paul Goldberger, *New York Times,* September 11, 1988, Architectural View column.

5. Kenneth Clark, *The Gothic Revival: An Essay in the History of Taste,* 3rd ed. (New York: Harper & Row, 1962), 9.

6. Quoted in Barbaralee Diamonstein, *American Architecture Now* (New York: Rizzoli, 1980), 126–27.

7. Leland M. Roth, *A Concise History of American Architecture* (New York: Harper & Row, 1979), 359.

8. Penelope Hunter-Stiebel, *Of Knights and Spires* (New York: Rosenberg & Stiebel Gallery, 1989), 8.

9. Martin Filler, "Gothic Getaway," *House and Garden* (June 1989): 105.

SELECTED BIBLIOGRAPHY

Addison, Agnes (Gilchrist). *Romanticism and the Gothic Revival.* New York: R. R. Smith, 1938.

Andrews, Wayne. *American Gothic: Its Origins, Its Trials, Its Triumphs.* New York: Random House, 1975.

Aslet, Clive, and Alan Powers. *The National Trust Book of the English House.* London: Viking, 1985.

Barton, Stuart. *Monumental Follies: An Exposition on the Eccentric Edifices of Britain.* Worthing: Lyle Publications, 1972.

Bence-Jones, Mark. *Burke's Guide to Country Houses, vol. I, Ireland.* London: Burke's Peerage, 1978.

Chambers, James. *The English House.* London: W. W. Norton, 1985.

Chippendale, Thomas. *The Gentleman & Cabinet-Maker's Director.* London: the author, 1754. Reprint, New York: Dover, 1977.

Clark, Kenneth. *The Gothic Revival: An Essay in the History of Taste.* New York: Holt, Rinehart & Winston, 1928. 3rd ed. New York: Harper & Row, 1962.

Cook, Olive. *The English House Through Seven Centuries.* New York: Overlook Press, 1983.

Cornack, Patrick. *English Cathedrals.* New York: Harmony Books, 1984.

Cram, Ralph Adams. *The Gothic Quest.* New York: Baker and Taylor, 1907.

_____. *My Life in Architecture.* Boston: Little, Brown, 1936.

Crook, Joseph Mordaunt. *William Burges and the High Victorian Dream.* Chicago: University of Chicago Press, 1981.

Davies, Jane B. *The Gothic Revival Style in America, 1830–1870.* Houston: Museum of Fine Arts, 1976.

Davis, Alexander Jackson. *Rural Residences Consisting of Designs, Original and Selected, for Cottages, Farm-Houses, Villas, and Village*

Churches. New York: the author, 1837, 1838. Reprint, New York: DaCapo Press, 1980.

Davis, Terence. *The Gothick Taste.* Rutherford, NJ: Fairleigh Dickinson University Press, 1975.

De Breffny, Brian. *Castles of Ireland.* London: Thames & Hudson, 1977.

_____, and Rosemary Ffolliott. *The Houses of Ireland.* New York: Viking Studio Press, 1975.

Decker, Paul. *Gothic Architecture, Decorated.* The author, 1759. Reprint, Farnsborough: Gregg International, 1968.

Diamonstein, Barbaralee. *American Architecture Now.* New York: Rizzoli, 1980.

Downing, Andrew Jackson. *The Architecture of Country Houses.* New York: D. Appleton, 1850. Reprint, New York: Dover, 1969.

_____. *Cottage Residences.* New York and London: Wiley and Putnam, 1842.

_____. *Rural Essays.* New York: George Putnam, 1853.

Downing, Antoinette, and Vincent Scully, Jr. *The Architectural Heritage of Newport, Rhode Island 1640–1914.* Cambridge: Harvard University Press, 1952.

Eastlake, Charles Locke. *A History of the Gothic Revival.* London: Longmans, Green and Co., 1872. Reprint, Leicester and New York: Leicester University Press and Humanities Press, 1970.

Girouard, Mark. "Alscot Park, Warwickshire." *Country Life* (May 15, 1958): 1065.

_____. "Cardiff Castle, Glamorganshire." *Country Life* (April 6, 1961): 760.

Goodwin, Francis. *Domestic Architecture.* London: the author, 1833. Supplement. London, printed for the author, 1835.

Halfpenny, William and John. *Chinese and Gothic Architecture Properly Ornamented.* London: printed for Robert Sayer, 1752.

Harbison, Peter, Homan Potterton, and Jeanne Sheehy. *Irish Art and Architecture from Prehistory to the Present.* London: Thames & Hudson, 1978.

Harris, Eileen. *British Architectural Books and Writers.* Cambridge and New York: Cambridge University Press, 1990.

Headley, Gwyn, and Wim Meulenkamp. *Follies: A National Trust Guide.* London: J. Cape, 1986.

Hewitt, Linda. *Chippendale and All the Rest: A View of English Antiques.* Cranbury, NJ: A. S. Barnes & Co., 1974.

Hunter-Stiebel, Penelope. *Of Knights and Spires.* New York: Rosenberg & Steibel Gallery, 1989.

Hussey, Christopher. *English Country Houses: Mid-Georgian, 1760–1800.* London: Country Life, 1956.

_____. "Houghton Lodge—I." *Country Life* (April 10, 1951): 1190.

_____. *The Picturesque: Studies in a Point of View.* London: Putnam, 1927. Reprint, 1967.

Jackson, John B. *The Necessity for Ruins.* Amherst: University of Massachusetts Press, 1980.

Jones, Barbara. *Follies and Grottoes.* London: Constable, 1953.

Lambton, Lucinda. *Beastly Buildings.* Boston: Atlantic Monthly Press, 1985.

Langley, B. & T. *Gothic Architecture Improved By Rules and Proportions. In Many Grand Designs.* London: I. & J. Taylor, 1742 (1747 edition, *Gothic Architecture Restored and Improved*). Reprint, Farnsborough: Gregg International Publications, 1968.

Lightolier, Thomas. *The Gentleman and Farmer's Architect.* Printed for Robert Sayers, 1762. Reprint, Farnsborough: Gregg International Publications, 1968.

Loth, Calder, and Julius Trousdale Sadler, Jr. *The Only Proper Style: Gothic Architecture in America.* New York: New York Graphic Society, 1975.

Loudon, John Claudius. *An Encyclopaedia of Cottage, Farm, and Villa Architecture and Furniture.* London: Longman, Brown, Green and Longman, 1833.

Maas, John. *The Gingerbread Age.* New York: Greenwich House, 1952.

McArdle, Alma and Deirdre. *Carpenter Gothic.* New York: Whitney Library of Design, 1978.

McCarthy, Michael. *The Origins of the Gothic Revival.* London and New Haven: Yale University Press, 1987.

Macaulay, James. *The Gothic Revival, 1745–1845.* Glasgow: Blackie, 1975.

Macaulay, Rose. *Pleasure of Ruins.* London: Weidenfeld and Nicolson, 1953.

Melville, Lewis. *The Life and Letters of William Beckford of Fonthill.* London: William Heinemann, 1910.

Mott, George, and Sally Aall. *Follies and Pleasure Gardens.* London: Pavilion Books, 1989.

Newton, Roger Hale. *Town & Davis: Architects.* New York: Columbia University Press, 1942.

Papworth, John. *Designs for Rural Residences.* London: R. Ackermann, 1818, 1832. Reprint, Farnsborough: Gregg International, 1971.

Pfeiffer, Walter, and Marianne Heron. *In the Houses of Ireland.* New York: Stewart, Tabori and Chang, 1988.

Pierson, William, Jr. *American Buildings and Their Architects.* Vol. 2, *Technology and the Picturesque: The Corporate and the Early Gothic Styles.* New York: Oxford University Press, 1978.

Plaw, John. *Ferme Ornée; or, Rural Improvements: A Series of Domestic and Ornamental Designs Calculated for Landscape and Picturesque Effects.* London: n.p., 1795.

Pryor, Kelli. "Back to Nature." *Avenue Magazine* (February 1989): 133.

Pugin, Augustus Claudius. *Examples of Gothic Architecture.* 3 vols. London: Bohn, 1831–38.

_____. *Specimens of Gothic Architecture,* 2 vols. London: M. A. Nattali, 1822–25.

Pugin, A. W. N. *Contrasts; or A Parallel Between the Noble Edifices of the 14th and 15th Centuries and Similar Buildings of the Present Day.* London: C. Dolman, 1836.

_____. *The True Principles of Pointed or Christian Architecture.* London: J. Weale, 1841.

Repton, Humphrey. *Observations on the Theory and Practice of Landscape Gardening.* London: J. Taylor, 1803.

Rickman, Thomas. *An Attempt to Discriminate the Styles of Architecture in England from the Conquest to the Reformation.* 2nd ed. London: Longman, Hurst, Rees, Orme, and Brown, 1819.

Roth, Leland M. *A Concise History of American Architecture.* New York: Harper & Row, 1979.

Ruskin, John. *The Seven Lamps of Architecture.* New York: John Wiley, 1849.

_____. *The Stones of Venice.* 3 vols. Boston: Estes and Lauriat, 1851–53.

Rykwert, Joseph. *On Adam's House in Paradise: The Idea of the Primitive Hut in Architectural History.* Cambridge, Mass.: M.I.T. Press, 1981.

Searing, Helen, David DeLong, and Robert A. M. Stern. *American Architecture—Innovation and Tradition.* New York: Rizzoli, 1986.

Simpson, Duncan. *Gothick 1720–1840.* England: Brighton Museum exhibition, 1975.

Sloan, Samuel. *The Model Architect.* Philadelphia: E. G. Jones, 1852, 1853. Reprinted as *Sloan's Victorian Buildings.* New York: Dover, 1980.

Stamp, Gavin, and Andre Goulancourt. *The English House, 1860–1914: The Flowering of English Domestic Architecture.* Boston: Faber and Faber, 1986.

Stanton, Phoebe. *Gothic Revival and American Church Architecture.* Baltimore: Johns Hopkins University Press, 1968.

_____. *Pugin.* New York: Viking Press, 1971.

Turnor, Reginold. *James Wyatt 1746–1813.* London: Art & Technics, 1950.

Vaux, Calvert. *Villas and Cottages.* 1855. Reprint, New York: Dover Publications, 1970.

Walker, Lester. *Tiny Houses.* Woodstock, NY: Overlook Press, 1987.

Walpole, Horace. Correspondence, Lewis Walpole Library, A Department of Yale University Library, Farmington, CT.

_____. *A Description of the Villa of Mr. Horace Walpole.* Twickenham, England: Strawberry Hill Press, Printed by Thomas Kirgate, 1784.

_____. *On Modern Gardening: An Essay by Horace Walpole.* 1780. Reprint, New York: Young Books, 1931.

Weiss, Ellen. *City in the Woods.* New York: Oxford University Press, 1987.

Wordsworth, Jonathan, Michael C. Jay, and Robert Woof. *William Wordsworth and the Age of English Romanticism.* New Brunswick, NJ: Rutgers University Press, 1987.

GLOSSARY

Apse   An extension at the east end of a church, usually semicircular, with a domed or vaulted ceiling.

Arch   A curved structural support that spans an opening.

Battlement   A parapet wall with notched edges.

Board and batten   A sheathing for frame buildings made up of wide vertical boards with narrow strips of wood covering the connecting joints.

Bracket   A projecting support under cornices, eaves, windows, and balconies used as a decorative element or for structural support.

Castellated   Having battlements and turrets like those of a medieval castle.

Chancel   The east end of a church, close to the altar, reserved for clergy and choir.

Corbel   A projecting block, usually of stone, that supports a beam or vault.

Cornice   A decorative molding, usually used as a terminal element.

Cottage orné   A rustic building popular in England in the late eighteenth and early nineteenth centuries, having gables, bay windows, clustered chimneys, and often thatched roofs, noted for its picturesque design.

Crenellation   Notched edge topping a tower wall.

Crocket   A carved, ornamental foliate projection used along the edges of pinnacles, spires, roofs, gables, etc.

Dado   The lower portion of an interior wall from floor to around waist height.

Dormer   A roof projection housing a window.

Fan vault   A highly decorated fanlike webbing of ribs within a vault, typical of the Perpendicular Gothic style.

Finial   An ornament, frequently leaflike, placed at the top of a tower, spire, or gable.

Flying buttress   A projecting masonry arch against an outer nave wall that strengthens the wall by applying counterthrust against the pressure of the vault.

Gable   A triangular form created by the juncture of two sloping roof lines.

Gothic arch   An arch that comes to a point at its apex.

Ha-ha   A ditch lined with stones to contain livestock, eliminating the need for a fence.

Hood molding   A projection, frequently rounded in form, extending across the top and part of the way down the sides of windows and doors to throw off rain. Also called a drip molding or a label molding.

Lancet   A narrow pointed window characteristic of early English Gothic.

Mullion   A support dividing a glazed window.

Nave   The main, axial volume of a church, usually flanked by side aisles.

Ogee arch   An arch introduced around 1300, composed of two opposing S curves that come to a point.

Oriel window   A bay window, generally extending from an upper story, supported by a projecting structure.

Pediment   A decorative element found above doors, windows, and fireplaces, or at the gable end of a building.

Pendant   An elongated ornamental projection.

Pier   A solid support designed for vertical pressure.

Pinnacle   A small turretlike Gothic structure, usually pointed, that is used as a decorative element topping a gable, buttress, etc.

Polychrome   Having a multicolored design, such as a pattern in masonry created with banding of contrasting colored brick or stone, typical of the High Victorian Gothic, 1865–1880.

Porte cochère   A covered areaway attached to a building, usually a large house, that originally was used to shelter carriages.

Quatrefoil   A decorative cloverlike pattern consisting of four lobes joined together.

Rib   A structural element or decorative projecting band in a vaulted ceiling.

Roundel   A round ornamental form.

Scagliola   Imitation marble, composed of cement or plaster with marble chips or other colored material.

Spandrel   The area, often triangular, between the side of an arch and the vertical supports enframing it.

Tracery   Decorative curvilinear pattern in the form of mullions supporting glass in a Gothic window or used for ornamenting screens, walls, buttresses, and gables.

Transept   A section of a church that intersects the nave at right angles, forming a cross and furnishing space for small side chapels.

Trefoil   A three-lobed cloverlike pattern.

Turret   A small tower sometimes extending from the corners of a building.

Vault   An arched ceiling of stone or wood.

Vergeboard   An ornamental carved board attached to the edge of a gable roof. Also called a bargeboard.

ILLUSTRATION CREDITS